Power through PRESENTATIONS

Andy Balser

Published by ECW Press
2120 Queen Street East, Suite 200, Toronto, Ontario, Canada M4E 1E2
416-694-3348 / info@ecwpress.com

LIBRARY AND ARCHIVES CANADA CATALOGUING IN PUBLICATION

Balser, Andy
Power through presentations : tips and tricks to build a
better slide deck / Andy Balser.

ISBN 978-1-55022-950-9
Also issued as 978-1-77090-350-0 (PDF) and 978-1-77090-348-7 (ePub)

1. Microsoft PowerPoint (Computer file). 2. Business
presentations—Graphic methods—Computer programs.
3. Multimedia systems in business presentations. I. Title.

P93.53.M534B35 2013   005.5'8   C2012-907531-0

Cover and text design: Carolyn McNeillie
Interior images: Andy Balser,
Earth Image — chrisroll / FreeDigitalPhotos.net
Author photo: Joanne Balser
Production: Troy Cunningham
Printing: United Graphics   1   2   3   4   5

ECW Press acknowledges the financial support of the Government of Canada through the Canada Book Fund for our publishing activities. The marketing of this book was made possible with the support of the Ontario Media Development Corporation.

PRINTED AND BOUND IN THE UNITED STATES

Power through PRESENTATIONS

Andy Balser

ECW

This book is dedicated to my lovely wife and three little daughters. It's possible that none of them will get around to reading it, but at least this page will give the girls something to color on.

Contents

Need slides now?

If you've picked up this book in a cold sweat because you need to pull together some handsome-looking slides by tomorrow, then fear not! I've got you covered. Just wander over to **www.powerthroughpresentations.com** and download some free slides that you can use right away. Once you've read through this book and become a slide ninja, you'll also have the chance to upload your best material to this website to offer it for sale.

"When a project is calm,

it is a beautiful thing."

Who is this book for?

This book was created just for you. You're not an elite presenter who's about to take the stage and call the world to action. You're a regular Joe or Jill who just needs a few slides you can review with co-workers. And half the time you're not even there in person, so you're either presenting over the phone or you've emailed the slide deck.

This book came to be because most other books about making PowerPoint® presentations are aimed at the presenter who's standing in front of a large audience, going on about some grand idea. And while these books have some great tips, they don't really hit the mark for the rest of us. With all the stuff you're expected to deliver on any given day, is making pretty slides even important? Yes, for two reasons:

1. We need to communicate complex ideas clearly and efficiently. People aren't willing to spend an entire week listening to you explain whatever it is you're working on.

2. The quality of your slides affects what people think about your work. If your slides look like garbage, people will assume the work that went into it is too.

This book offers some everyday tips, tricks, and templates for making great slides. At a minimum, you'll make slides that suck less than they do now.

Is this book for me?

Here's how to tell. The facing page shows what a lot of those other books might try to teach you about building slides. It features a Zen-like minimalism, imagery that complements the message, and a bunch of other stuff you probably don't want to spend time reading about.

If presenting something like this at work would get you a response to the effect of, "That's great, hippie, now tell me why your project has gone off the rails," then this book is for you.

11

The Basics

Choosing what to use

DON'T BE A DUMB-ASS, ONLY PRESENT WHAT YOUR AUDIENCE NEEDS

Let's be clear about one thing: the people you're making the slides for aren't there to see, hear, or read about you. They just need to get information quickly and clearly. It doesn't really matter whether it's you delivering it or you've trained a talking donkey to do it.

If you take nothing else away from this book, take this: you must understand exactly what your audience needs to know and then let that be your guide in choosing what to include on your slides. If you find yourself thinking, "But I spent 50 hours analyzing the last three years of sales data and they should know how hard that was," then give yourself a shake and refocus. The only thing you're there to do is address what your audience needs. If that analysis is on target, that's great, it's in. If it doesn't help you deliver what your audience needs, then too bad, it's out. Creating a presentation is a bit like carving a stone sculpture.

Try not to get too hung up on the big chunks of rock that are falling to the floor; just make sure the end result is great.

So, right off the bat, figure out why you're there. It could be for a number of reasons, such as:

- "They need an update on the status of my project";
- "We need to make a decision";
- "I need to convince them to do something."

Consider starting your presentation by telling everyone exactly what you want them to walk away with. This will ground their thought processes so that, as you go through your material, you build toward an established goal. Here's a quick example:

PRODUCT REVENUE IS DOWN FOR THE THIRD YEAR IN A ROW

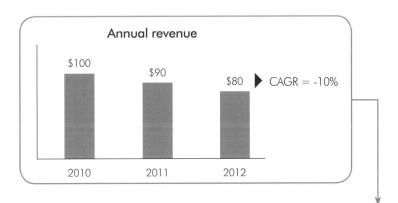

Outcomes for today
- Decide whether or not to exit this business
  - If we exit, what will our divestiture plan be?
  - If we stay the course, who will lead the turnaround?

If you were a sniper, the gray box at the bottom of this slide would be your crosshairs. Any material that doesn't directly help answer these questions should not appear in your presentation.

So how can you develop the crosshairs for your presentation? Start by asking yourself (and others) questions about who your audience is, what decisions your presentation might help them make, and what else they do when they're not taking in a riveting presentation by you. You can approach these questions in a similar way by asking yourself what you want people to think when they see your material, how you want them to feel about it, and what you want them to do once it's all over. Use your answers to come up with the two or three outcomes that your presentation needs to accomplish (i.e., your crosshairs). Since you're a clever person, you can probably come up with your own list of questions, but here are a few examples to get you started:

- Why does each person want to see/read my presentation?
- What decisions will my information help them make?
- What are some of my audience's preconceived notions, which I might need to overcome?

- Are audience members involved with other projects that might be affected by my project or knowledge?
- How does each person's job performance get measured at the end of the year? How can my presentation help others meet their performance targets?
- Who will be the most likely person to raise questions? Is there anything that I can include to help anticipate questions? Can I send this person anything beforehand to avoid being taken off track?
- What are the company's or team's biggest priorities? What parts of my initiative link to these?

There's a reason that everyone isn't the CEO

As you're plotting and scheming to develop a great presentation, it might help to keep in mind what part of the corporate ladder you're developing slides for. Different levels typically have different needs. Each situation will vary, but here are a couple of examples of the types of concerns some of these different groups might have:

Frontline
- How does this help me do my job better?
- Does this help me understand the bigger picture?

Middle management
- How will this impact my team?
- Does it inform any decisions I might have to make?
- Does this keep me aware of things that are important to the company?

Senior management
- How does this help me make investment decisions?
- How will this differentiate us in the market?
- What impact will this have on financials and shareholder value?

"Sorry, baby, it's not you. It's me."

There's a good reason that your company pays you the bags and bags of money it does. It's because you know stuff. Probably a lot of stuff. However, the audience isn't there to be in awe of all the wonderful things you know. Yet going on and on about the stuff we know is one of the most common traps that we fall into when putting a presentation together. Breaking your emotional attachment to the work you've put into something or the expertise you've developed is one of the best ways you can improve your presentations. Don't worry about trying to show that you're the smartest kid in the class or that you're the hardest working bee in the hive. If you deliver what your audience needs, the rest will shine through. So as emotionally attached as you might feel to some of your work, detaching yourself will help you build a stronger focus on your audience.

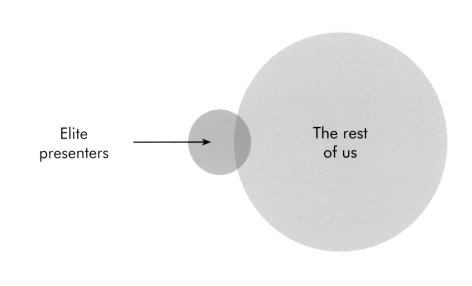

Elite
presenters

The rest
of us

Delivery options

WE'RE NOT ALL AL GORE

Most of those other books on creating pretty slides were probably written by smart, well-intentioned people whose mothers love them. The trouble is, they usually assume you're about to jump onstage in front of an audience full of strong-willed people whose opinions you need to change. And while that might help elite presenters, the rest of us usually just need to get our stuff into slides so we can review it with people at work.

You're likely to use one (or more) of four delivery methods:

1. You're nowhere in sight because you emailed it (as a document).
2. You're presenting in person.
3. You're presenting over the phone (perhaps with a shared desktop).
4. Some combination of the above.

One of the most common presentation crimes is trying to create a single deck that can be used for all of these scenarios. That's a bit like trying to eat a steak dinner with a Swiss Army knife. Sure, you can do it, but you're not using the right tool for the job so it's going to get messy.

Which one of the four scenarios will you run into the most often? Number four, of course. So don't try to create a Swiss Army knife to deal with this; rather, create the knife, spoon, and fork separately. "Forget it, I'm not creating more than one slide deck," you might be shouting. But don't slam the book shut just yet.

Let's start by taking a look at number one, since you usually end up emailing the presentation to someone. Here are a few tips:

- Explain what the major point of each slide is. This is often done with a "so what?" box at the bottom.

- Use full sentences. You don't need people putting extra brainpower into interpreting your sentence fragments.

Here's an example of what these two concepts might look like on a slide.

As much as possible, try to minimize the use of business speak like "We're experiencing a paradigm shift that key stakeholders must address in order to preserve our competitive positioning." Say what? What planet did you come from? Use plain language, as though you're explaining it to a normal earthling.

Simplify your charts and data. Don't include numbers that aren't relevant to your main point. For example, take a look at the dog's breakfast on this slide. This was inspired by a real slide used for a review with a senior executive at a 30,000-person corporation.[1] This isn't math class, so you don't always need to show your work (although the level of detail your audience needs will vary). The slide on the next page is a revision that just focuses on the main points. The key is to do more than just a simple data transfer. Provide some insight.

2010 YEAR-END FINANCIAL RESULTS

MONTH ACTUAL	BUDGET	OUTLOOK	VARIANCES PRIOR MO	PRIOR YR	PRIOR YR %	CURRENT MONTH	YTD ACTUAL	BUDGET	OUTLOOK	PRIOR YR	PRIOR YR %	BUDGET	OUTLOOK
44.3	-0.8	-0.8	-0.3	2.7	3%	Internal gross manufacturing costs	512.1	0.3	-3.8	37.0	4%	512.4	508.3
-13.3	-0.7	1.4	-2.9	1.7	9%	Internal manufacturing capex flows	-176.9	2.2	3.6	-7.1	-2%	-174.6	-173.3
31.0	-1.4	1.1	-3.1	4.5	7%	Net internal manufacturing costs	335.1	2.6	0.2	29.8	5%	337.7	335.0
39.9	-16.4	-6.1	-4.7	0.1	0%	External gross manufacturing costs	355.1	-1.5	2.1	96.6	12%	353.6	357.3
27.5	12.2	5.5	3.9	-3.5	-6%	External manufacturing capex flows	-236.7	-13.6	-2.6	-105.5	-18%	250.3	-239.3
12.5	-4.2	-0.6	-0.7	-3.4	-22%	Net external manufacturing costs	118.5	-15.1	-0.5	-8.9	-5%	103.3	117.9
14.4	-3.7	-1.4	-0.9	-2.5	-12%	Labor costs	163.0	-17.3	-2.2	2.6	1%	145.6	160.7
98.7	-20.9	-8.3	-5.9	0.3	0%	Total Gross	1030.2	18.5	-3.8	136.2	7%	1011.6	1026.3
57.9	-9.3	-0.7	-4.9	-1.4	-2%	Total Net	616.6	-29.9	-2.9	23.6	2%	586.7	613.7
10.5	1.9	0.6	-1.0	1.6	10%	Capex flows	120.3	151.9	2.7	8.6	5%	-105.0	117.7
47.4	-7.4	-0.1	-5.8	0.2	0%	EBITDA impact (gross)	496.2	-14.5	-0.2	32.2	3%	481.7	496.1
40.3	-6.3	-0.1	-5.0	0.1	0%	EBITDA impact (net)	421.8	-12.3	-0.1	25.8	3%	409.5	421.6

becomes ⟶

---

[1] This example was inspired by Daryl Storey.

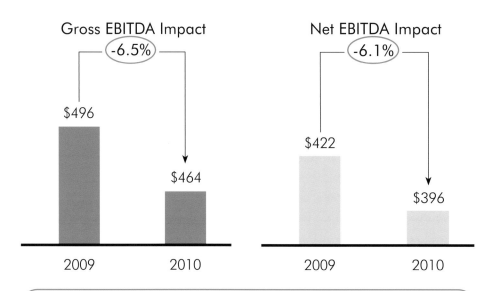

Sometimes that dog's breakfast is a template that you're expected to use and shouldn't deviate from. If that's the case, consider putting the pretty slide in front of it so you can deliver the key messages clearly before jumping into that other mess, which risks taking you off course.

Let's get back to that multiple-slide-deck thing you've been worrying about. If you're going to be in person and speaking directly to your audience, you want an absolute minimum amount of content on your slides. Why? Because we're not that smart. People have trouble reading and listening at the same time (more on that on page 112 in the "How we process information" section). If your slide has a lot of text or data on it, your audience will either be reading the slide or listening to you — not both.

For presentations delivered in person, slides are typically designed to do one or more of three things:

1. Help reinforce a major point you're trying to make.
2. Quickly illustrate something that would be complex to explain.
3. Remind the audience of what you're talking about after they've returned from a few moments of daydreaming.

Once you've made your "emailing slides," the quickest way to create the ones you're going to be speaking to is to start deleting. If you're going to be there to explain it anyway, you don't have to make people try to read the slides for themselves at the same time.

Let's take the two slides from above. Here's one way to reuse both of them if you're presenting in person:

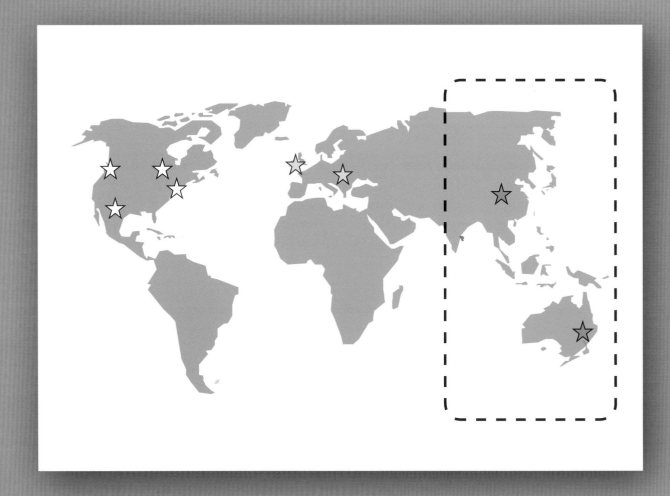

24

$396M

-6%

Too simple? No way! If you're going to be there explaining the story anyway, you don't need to describe the content, too. Just throw one of these bad boys up on the screen and then wait a couple of steamboats for people to absorb it. This will create enough curiosity that people might actually pay attention to what you're going to say. And the slides won't be a distraction once you start talking. And they help reinforce the major points you're trying to make. And they take hardly any time at all to make, so you have more time for that game of solitaire you were playing.

But what about when you're hunched over in your cubicle, explaining your slides over the phone? Surprise, surprise, using a hybrid of the other two approaches is a good way to go. This means you'll need to find a balance between:

1. In-person minimalism: when the audience is on the phone, there are even more distractions for them (emails coming in, people stopping by their desks, shiny objects outside the window), so the in-person slides that have almost no text won't provide enough detail.

2. Emailed detail: If you use the slides you created to be emailed, then you're back in the boat where people are trying to read while you're trying to get them to listen to you.

A nice, quick way to strike the right balance is to reveal your material gradually by layering details on each new slide. This is called a slide build. You can spoon-feed the details, pausing to explain things that need discussion and quickly going through the stuff that doesn't. On the facing page is an example of what a slide build might look like.

Notice how we didn't explain how to use animation to build these slides? That's because the vast majority of people hate it, whether it's a text box that swoops onto a slide from nowhere or it's a dancing paperclip that tries to help you as you type.

You got all that? Good. This section provided some of the ground rules for creating slides for the delivery methods you're most likely to use. But doing all the work yourself sucks. So grab your ski mask and a baseball bat, and let's look at how to steal some stuff.

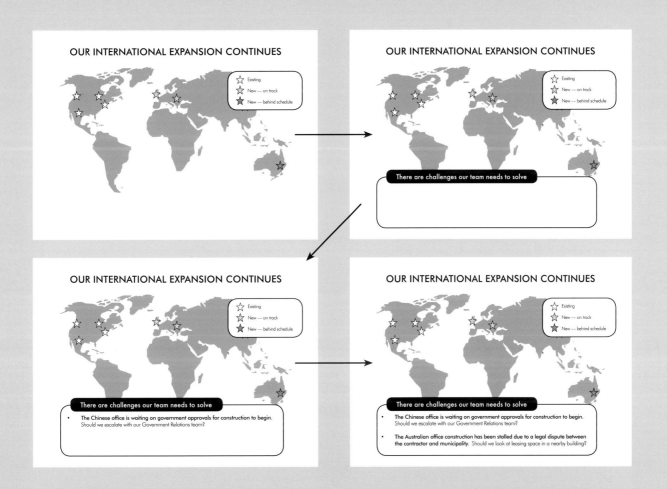

Get Organized

Finding inspiration

"GOOD ARTISTS COPY, GREAT ARTISTS STEAL"

This is a quote that was stolen from Steve Jobs. And he stole it from Picasso. So don't worry about stealing, you're in good company.

In your day-to-day work life, you're likely to come across some presentations that are way better than what you put together. So rather than throwing yourself a pity party at your desk, whimpering about how lousy you are and how great that other person is, just toughen up, channel your inner thug, and go steal the stuff that you think is so great.

Before anyone thinks they can interpret this section as a call to violate copyright or intellectual property laws, please, just chill out. The main message here is to grab inspiration when it hits you. Don't reuse someone else's material and try to pass it off as your own: that's what's referred to as a CLM (career-limiting move). Rather, make sure you're learning from the approaches that others use in order to make your own slides better.

Over the course of a given month, you probably produce a lot of slides. So if you want to be able to make better slides without a lot of effort, take a second to create a folder on your computer labeled "presentation archive," or some such thing. Any time you find a slide that you like, grab it and put it in this folder. Try to save only the slide or two that wowed you, not the entire deck. This will help you avoid having to sift through a heap of stuff in order to find something useful.

You'll often have slide decks sent to you, so it's easy to add slides from those to your loot bag. But what if you're sitting in a conference room and you see a magical slide appear onscreen that you might not have emailed to you afterwards? Chances are your cell phone or smartphone has a camera. (If it doesn't, then you have a pressing issue to attend to.) Assuming the material onscreen isn't sensitive or private, go ahead and take a picture. And rather than acting like you're a member of the paparazzi, you might even want to preface your picture-taking by asking something like, "There's some great stuff here that would be valuable to my team, do you mind if I grab a quick photo to review later?"

If you're sitting at your desk watching someone else's slide through remote desktop sharing, it's even easier. Most computers allow you to grab a picture of whatever you see on your screen and then save it as an image. You should be able to capture it with one of these combinations of keystrokes:

- Prnt Scrn
- Ctrl + Prnt Scrn
- Fn + Prnt Scrn
- Command + Shift +3 (on a Mac)

There you go. Three easy ways to be the Captain Jack Sparrow of slide presentations.

START WITH SOME PETTY THEFT

But what if you work with a bunch of primates who never create good slides? Fear not, this section has some stuff you can steal. Lucky for you, it was stolen from people who are pretty good at making slides.

The next few sections show how to illustrate different concepts with eye-catching visuals. This will help you cut back on the amount of text while delivering crisp, clear messages more efficiently, whether you're emailing the slides or presenting them in person. To avoid scaring you, we'll start slowly, with some stuff you've probably already seen. But by the end, be sure to have your seatbelt buckled for the wild ride that is awesome PowerPoint® templates.

Tools for communicating status

Back to kindergarten for this first one. Traffic lights are a simple way to show how something is doing. You usually don't even need to include a legend, since it's generally understood that:

 Everything is on track.

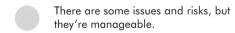 There are some issues and risks, but they're manageable.

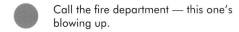 Call the fire department — this one's blowing up.

Here's what it might look like on a slide:

ACTION IS NEEDED TO DRIVE SOME INVENTORY LEVELS

Status	Region	Notes
🔘	North America	Inventory levels on target
🔘	South America	Inventory levels on target
🔘	Asia-Pacific	1 of 8 factories behind schedule, extra shift to be added to catch up
🔘	Europe	Inventory levels on target
🔴	Africa	Labor disruption driving severe inventory shortages

DECISION
Should we increase European capacity to compensate for the challenge in Africa?

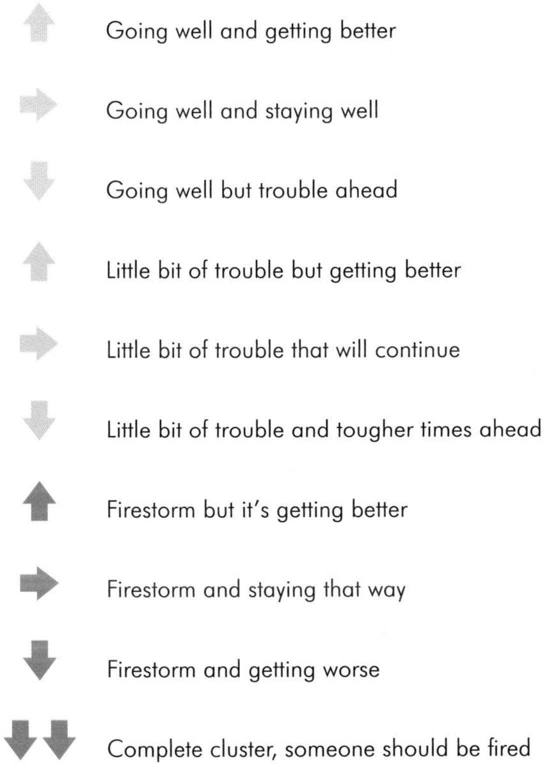

⬆ Going well and getting better

➡ Going well and staying well

⬇ Going well but trouble ahead

⬆ Little bit of trouble but getting better

➡ Little bit of trouble that will continue

⬇ Little bit of trouble and tougher times ahead

⬆ Firestorm but it's getting better

➡ Firestorm and staying that way

⬇ Firestorm and getting worse

⬇⬇ Complete cluster, someone should be fired

Tools for communicating trends

One step beyond simple green, yellow, and red is the addition of an element of time to indicate which way something is trending. A simple way to do this is by using colored arrows rather than colored circles, which tell the audience what the current status is (the color) as well as which way the status is heading (the direction of the arrow). At left is the generally understood meaning of each option.

Not started

Roughly 12.5% done

Roughly 25% done

Roughly 37.5% done

Roughly 50% done

Roughly 62.5% done

Roughly 75% done

Roughly 87.5% done

Complete

Tools for communicating progress

A slick way to show a project's level of completeness is to use something called Harvey Balls (insert your own inappropriate joke here). Think of these little fellas as mini pie charts that give a rough sense for how complete something is. They're usually used to show an approximate percentage of completion in increments of either 12.5 or 25 percent. The most common variations are shown above.

But how do you create and edit these mystical little Harvey Balls? Fear not, they're pretty easy to make. Just go to the Insert menu, choose the Shape tool, and then choose the shape that looks like a pie with a piece missing. Once you insert it, the shape will display two little yellow diamonds that you can click and drag to create the size of slice you'd like. After you get the slice of pie that represents the right amount of progress you want to show, just put it on top of a regular circle, and boom! There's your Harvey Ball. You can then change the shading and borders as you would any other shape. Here's a quick "how to" to get you started:

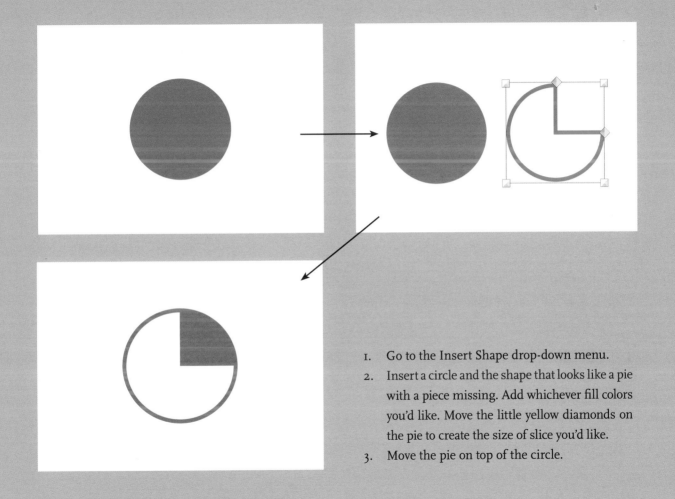

1. Go to the Insert Shape drop-down menu.
2. Insert a circle and the shape that looks like a pie with a piece missing. Add whichever fill colors you'd like. Move the little yellow diamonds on the pie to create the size of slice you'd like.
3. Move the pie on top of the circle.

Tools for communicating relationships

No, not that kind of relationship. Think dependency. Okay, not that kind of dependency. Just think of a connection between two different things.

One relationship that we often need to represent in a slide is an overlap between two things. A Venn diagram does this pretty well. Here's an example of what it might look like.

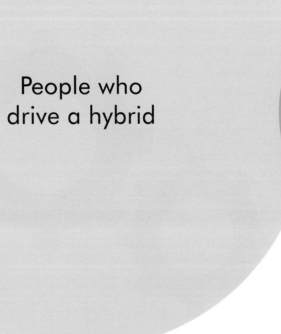

People who
drive a hybrid

People who
burn their own
garbage

Very few people
do both

If you want to show a causal relationship (i.e., show how changing something has an impact on something else), use gears. These are nice, since turning one turns the others in different directions. You can show how different things are influenced either positively or negatively. Here's an example.

Want to feel like an engineer without having to go through the four years of college not having a date? See the opposite page to learn how to build your very own gears in a slide:

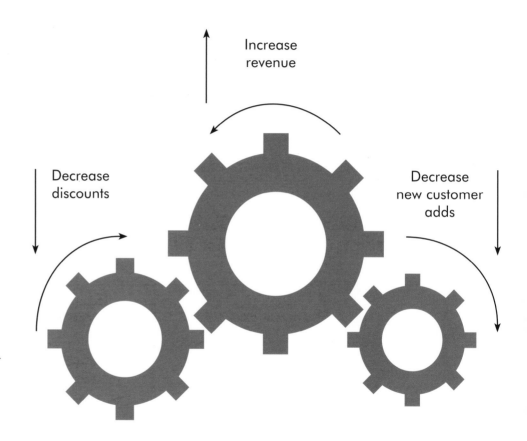

Increase revenue

Decrease discounts

Decrease new customer adds

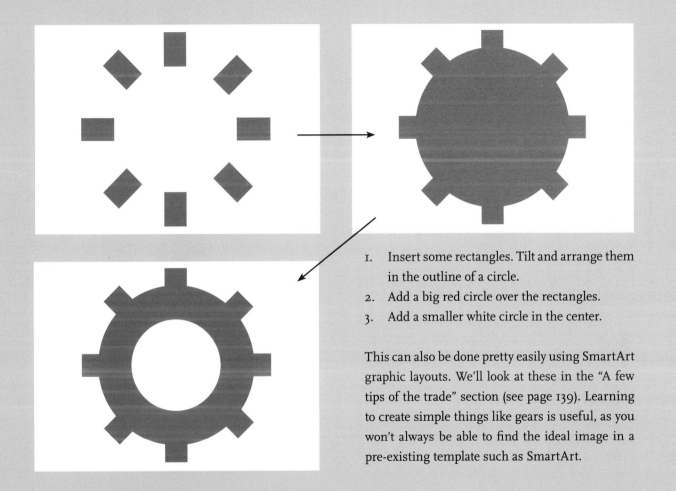

1. Insert some rectangles. Tilt and arrange them in the outline of a circle.
2. Add a big red circle over the rectangles.
3. Add a smaller white circle in the center.

This can also be done pretty easily using SmartArt graphic layouts. We'll look at these in the "A few tips of the trade" section (see page 139). Learning to create simple things like gears is useful, as you won't always be able to find the ideal image in a pre-existing template such as SmartArt.

Constraints or limiting factors

Sometimes, despite your best efforts, there's something that's messing up your project. If it's acting like a choke point, you can illustrate the concept by using an image of a funnel. Usually a regular old funnel will do the trick, but here's a fancy-schmancy double-ended funnel.

But how can you create such a sexy hourglass figure? It's really just a matter of overlaying some inverted triangles under an oval. The next page shows the basic steps . . .

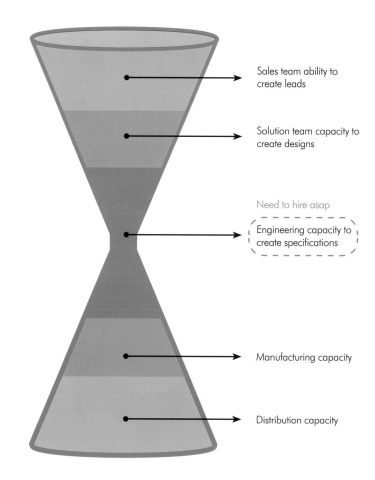

Sales team ability to create leads

Solution team capacity to create designs

Need to hire asap

Engineering capacity to create specifications

Manufacturing capacity

Distribution capacity

1. Start with a triangle.

2. Add a darker triangle on top.

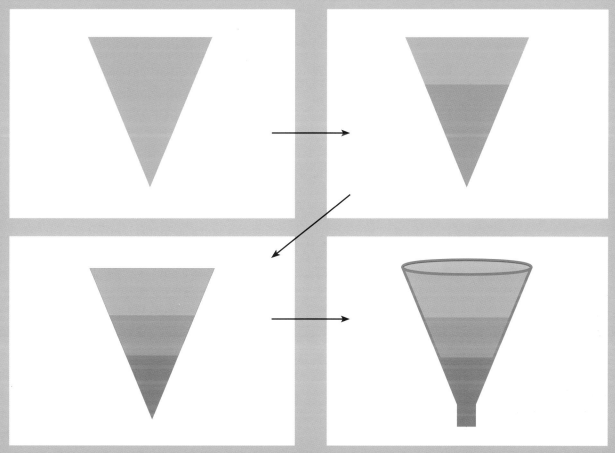

3. Keep adding darker triangles until you have all the layers you need.

4. Add an ellipse at the top, a rectangle at the bottom, and two thick lines down each side.

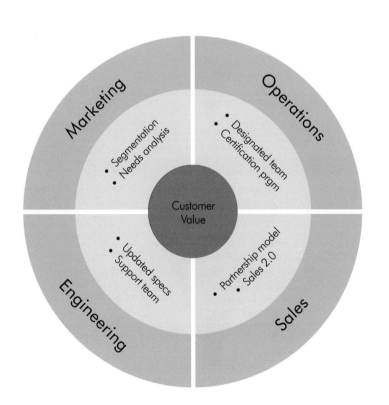

Summarizing what it's all about

Sometimes you need a way to bring everything you're working on into a single visual. The good ol' bull's-eye works well for that kind of thing. You can design it any way you want and here are a few suggestions to help get you started:

- The outermost rings tend to be high-level concepts (i.e., business units, departments, overarching strategies).
- The inner rings often describe the outer rings in more detail (i.e., specific tactics).
- The bull's-eye in the center is your main objective.

You can create a bull's-eye simply by overlaying some circles. You can then create the slices of the pie by adding white lines. Nothing to it for a smart kid like you.

Those are some pretty basic ways to create visuals that will illustrate different concepts. To help get you started, a few great templates can be downloaded from www.powerthroughpresentations.com. They're all pretty straightforward, and you can add them to your bag of tricks. Now let's pull this all together and get our hands on some bigger loot.

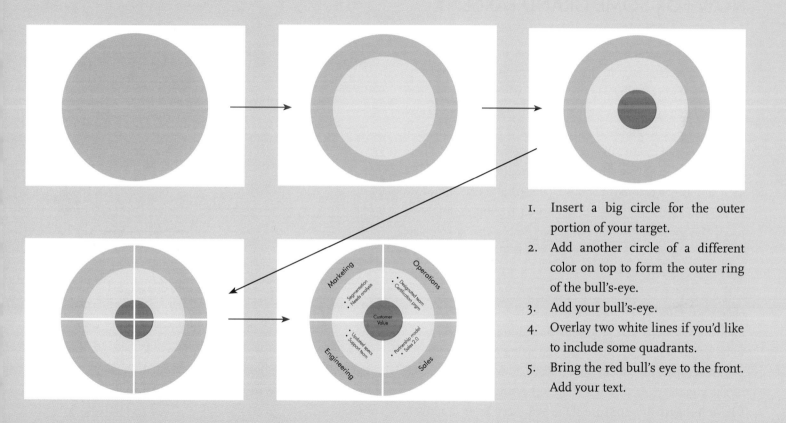

1. Insert a big circle for the outer portion of your target.
2. Add another circle of a different color on top to form the outer ring of the bull's-eye.
3. Add your bull's-eye.
4. Overlay two white lines if you'd like to include some quadrants.
5. Bring the red bull's eye to the front. Add your text.

NOW FOR SOME GRAND LARCENY

Now that you've got a few misdemeanors under your belt by borrowing stuff shown in the previous section, it's time to go after something a bit bigger and badder. We'll be taking a look at a few one-page templates that you can use to create useful slides. Again, you can use these as inspiration — and be sure to twist, turn, and modify them to suit your own purposes. There are headings in this section that identify the typical uses for each template (e.g., Project Status Update), but consider these to be just one of the many possible ways each template might be used. The approach used in the Project Status Update template may, for example, be a good way for you to show progress on a sales campaign instead.

Logical flow

Showing the steps in a process is something that often needs to be described in presentations, and using a bunch of bullet points is a painful way of going about it. A much nicer way of showing steps is through shapes that are called chevrons. Chevrons help paint a picture of the flow that's being described.

Here's a quick example:

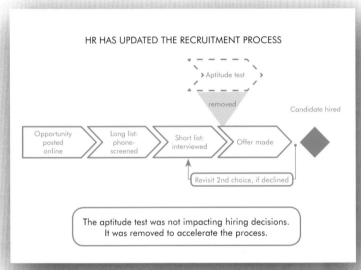

This is a pretty easy way to walk people through the flow of how something is done. Two chevron shapes are available in PowerPoint® software, and you can find them in the Shapes menu.

Process overviews

The world of process improvement is exhilarating. It's surprising they're not making more movies about it. But if Hollywood isn't beating down your door to tell your story for you, you can use templates like these to do it yourself.

You might need to describe how a process or system works for a number of reasons. Sometimes you're showing what needs to be changed. Sometimes you're demonstrating how multiple teams work together. And sometimes you're explaining how royally messed up something is.

Whatever your reason, be clear on the main purpose of the discussion, and approach it from your audience's perspective. (If you're not sure how to figure that out, go back and reread the "Don't be a dumb-ass" section on pages 14–17.) Many process diagrams are built as flow charts and display way too much information. Try to boil down your slide to the key teams and interactions that highlight the main points you're trying to make.

One simple approach is to create swim lanes for each of the areas you want to show an interaction between. Here's an example that demonstrates how an escalation process is used to support technical issues for customers:

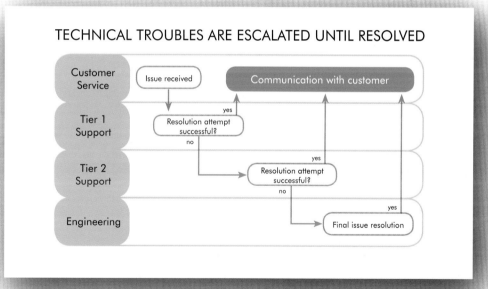

45

Sometimes our lives would be so much easier without those darn customers, and maybe you need to frame a discussion on something more fascinating, such as IT systems. You could modify the above template to look like the diagram to the right.

The concept is the same in both cases. Create some swim lanes for each part of the business involved in the interactions you want to discuss, and then overlay the flow of the story you're describing on top of them.

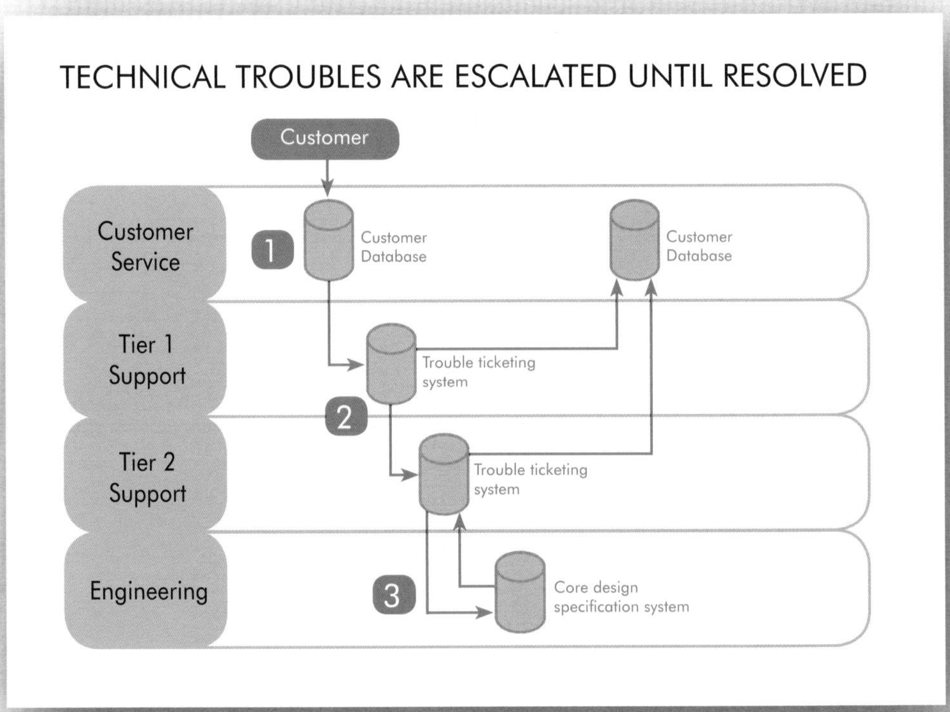

TECHNICAL TROUBLES ARE ESCALATED UNTIL RESOLVED

Customer

Customer Service

1   Customer Database   Customer Database

Tier 1 Support

Trouble ticketing system

2

Tier 2 Support

Trouble ticketing system

Engineering

3   Core design specification system

Template: project status update

There's a bunch of ways to provide a project update: some are pretty and some look like you had a few too many the night before. The most common project updates use some form of a Gantt chart, which is a diagram that shows the timelines of the various streams of activity. Here are a couple of things to keep in mind before you put pen to paper (or cursor to screen, as the case may be):

- What does your audience need? Are they there to help you solve problems? Or do they just need to know the status of your project because it will have an impact on other projects? Be clear on this so that you can provide the right details (and leave out the irrelevant ones).

- Which aspects of your project are most important? This might include things like budget, timelines, or the status of different parts of the project. Keeping the first point in mind, only include the parts that are relevant.

- Does your audience already know what your project is about? Should you provide a quick overview first? If you do need to write a short description, bounce it off someone else to see if it makes sense. When you're neck-deep into a project, it's easy to take too much for granted and explain it in a way that won't make sense to people who are learning about it for the first time.

- Although the needs of audiences will vary, most require a future-looking view of a project. While it might be tempting to fire up a stogie, kick back, and celebrate the project's accomplishments as well as your own successes (i.e. look back), most audiences will want to hear about what's coming next (i.e. look ahead). You might throw in a couple of examples of successes to strengthen your credibility, but don't make your presentation a party about you. Similarly, you might need to explain why something either didn't go or isn't going well. Don't drag your audience kicking and screaming through all the painful details of what you went through; rather, explain it in such a way that you're looking forward and outlining what you will do to overcome the current debacle — and avoid it occurring again down the road.

Here's a good example of a project update that uses a handful of concepts from the last section to do a number of things, including:

1. Break the project into four discrete streams.
2. Provide an indication of the status of each stream.
3. Provide a sense of how complete each stream is.
4. Look into the future and show a roadmap for how to get there.
5. Highlight a major risk that needs to be discussed.

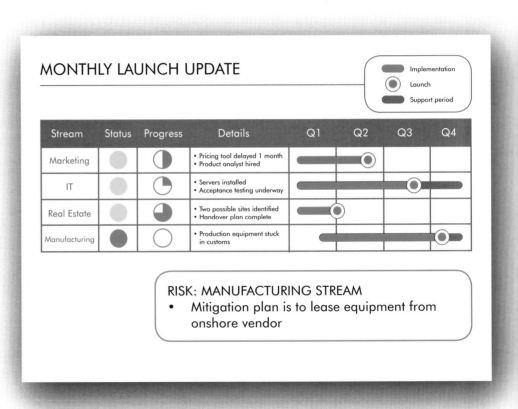

MONTHLY LAUNCH UPDATE

Implementation
Launch
Support period

Stream	Status	Progress	Details	Q1	Q2	Q3	Q4
Marketing			• Pricing tool delayed 1 month • Product analyst hired				
IT			• Servers installed • Acceptance testing underway				
Real Estate			• Two possible sites identified • Handover plan complete				
Manufacturing			• Production equipment stuck in customs				

RISK: MANUFACTURING STREAM
• Mitigation plan is to lease equipment from onshore vendor

Template for presenting a business opportunity or strategic overview

One of the most common presentation formats for describing a business opportunity is something called a SWOT analysis. Settle down, GI Joe, we're not talking about SWAT, we're talking about SWOT. Pretty much any Business 101 textbook will show this two-by-two matrix with quadrants labeled Strengths, Weaknesses, Opportunities, and Threats. It's a decent way to describe the aspects of the company (strengths and weaknesses) and compare it to what's going on externally (opportunities and threats). Here's an example of how a SWOT analysis can be used:

SHOULD WE ENTER THE WIDGET MARKET?

	Reasons for doing it	Concerns with doing it
Internal	**STRENGTHS** • Lowest cost base in the industry • Extensive patent assets • Product well positioned	**WEAKNESSES** • Collective agreement with unionized members expiring • COO position still vacant • Merger integration not complete
External	**OPPORTUNITIES** • Several under-served niches in the market • Major outages by competitors created general market dissatisfaction	**THREATS** • Regulatory intervention is an uncertain risk • Market growth has stagnated in recent years

Template for describing a journey or dependencies

Something called an Ishikawa diagram might come in handy if you're looking for a way to group your thoughts and show how they all work toward a common goal. Even if this template isn't ideal for your purpose, just using the term "Ishikawa" will render your audience mildly confused, making you seem enlightened and intellectual.

The nice thing about this template is that you can create as many branches as you have major categories. Under each branch you can then list a few of your supporting points as twigs. It can also make a good intro slide, providing an overview of the journey, and then with the rest of the slides in your deck, you can dive deeper into each branch or twig.

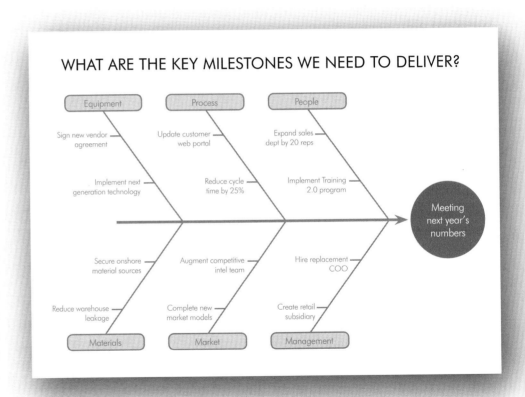

Template for separating yourself from the competition

A strategic canvas is a really great tool for showing how your strategy is going to separate you from the competition. Oh yeah, this is good stuff. Just saying the words "strategic canvas" makes it sound like you know what's going on. This template is taken from a book called *Blue Ocean Strategy*, which was written by two smarty-pants named W. Chan Kim and Renée Mauborgne.

It's essentially a graph on which you list the major aspects of how you compete (or what customers want) along the horizontal axis. Then you create a line graph that shows how you and your competitors rate against each aspect.

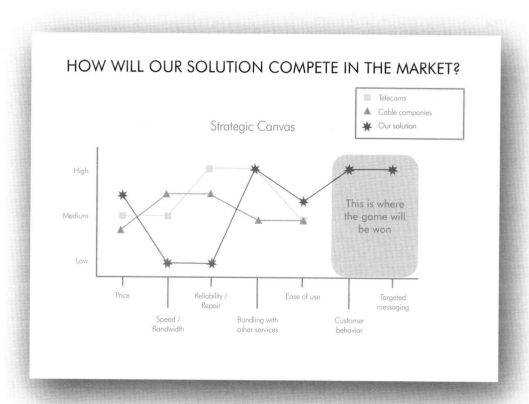

HOW WILL OUR SOLUTION COMPETE IN THE MARKET?

Telecoms
Cable companies
Our solution

Strategic Canvas

High
Medium
Low

This is where the game will be won

Price
Speed / Bandwidth
Reliability / Repair
Bundling with other services
Ease of use
Customer behavior
Targeted messaging

The hall of shame

Now that we've gone through a handful of tricks you can use, let's take a look at some images to avoid. If you find yourself reaching for any of these, please stop: you run the risk of having the 1990s call you and ask for their inspirational posters back.

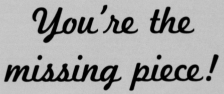
You're the missing piece!

Let's collaborate!

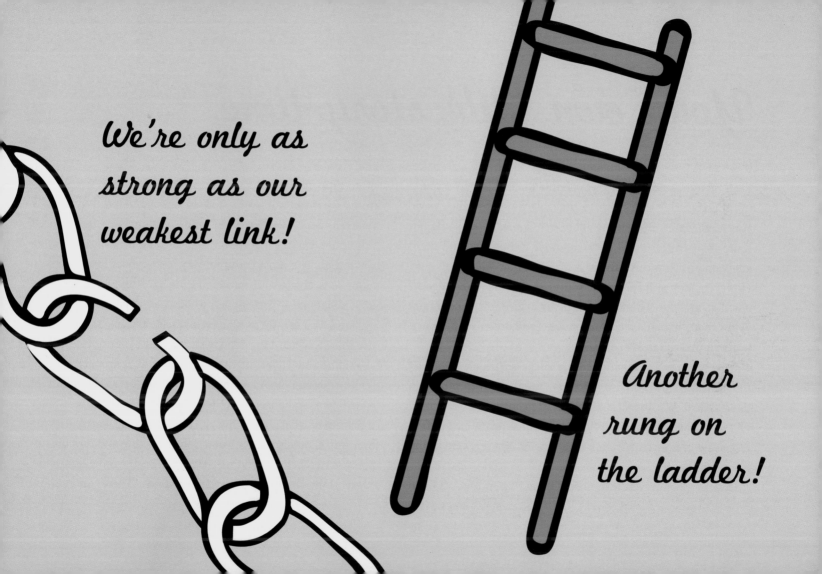

Your own little story-time

Even though you might not yet be the Michael Jordan of making PowerPoint® slides, you're probably clever in other ways. You might know everything there is to know about some obscure topic in the world of business or technology, and there are people at your company who need to know what you know. However, they probably want you to share this knowledge in less than an hour. This section is going to give you some frameworks that will help take your thoughts and organize them in a way that makes sense to others.

Whether you are emailing your slides so people can read them on their own or you are reviewing them with others in person, bear in mind that people like to consume information in a nice, orderly fashion. It helps them understand how different pieces of information link together and where you're trying to take the story.

However, before you take one of these frameworks and run off to whip up slides that are beautiful works of art, start by outlining what you want your story to look like. This is commonly referred to as "storyboarding" your presentation, and while it might not feel like it at first, it is one of the biggest time-savers you'll find. The most common way to storyboard your presentation is to create your entire slide deck using just the titles of each slide (and if you happen to have some pre-baked content on hand, you can throw that on a few slides too). You can then use this storyboard to refine what the flow of your presentation should be and what content you should add or drop. If you can, review the storyboard with other people (peers, members of your future audience) to get feedback on your approach. Since the death of a beautiful slide is truly something worth grieving over, you should try to lock down the structure and flow of your presentation before building the details on any individual slide.

All right, back to story frameworks. There are several

approaches to consider, some that are general purpose and some that are designed for a specific situation. Let's start with an easy one.

Framework: the Five Ws

You're probably already familiar with these, given that you've made it through at least a few grades at school. They're often called the "Five Ws" or the "Five Ws and one H." Using who, what, where, when, why, and how is a pretty simple way to organize and structure the flow of your information, especially when you're trying to introduce a new concept or project to the audience. Not only have these little words been used extensively in journalism and police investigations, they're also something just about everyone has seen before. You don't have to use all six every time. Stick to the ones that are useful. Here's a quick example that uses four of them.

I keep six honest serving-men
(They taught me all I knew);
Their names are
What
and Why and When
And How and Where
and Who.

— Rudyard Kipling

PERSONNEL PLANNER PROJECT (3P)
Overview

WHAT	OVERVIEW OF THE PROJECT
WHY	THE DRIVING FORCES
HOW	KEY CHANGES BEING DELIVERED
WHEN	THE IMPLEMENTATION PLAN

OVERVIEW OF THE PROJECT

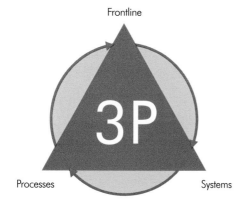

- The Personnel Planner Project (3P) is a comprehensive resource management system in customer service

- 3P will upgrade the IT systems, ordering processes, and training for frontline representatives

- Capex: $2.2M

- ROI: 26%

WHY THE DRIVING FORCES

- Revenue in the customer service department has stagnated over the past 12 months.

- Legacy IT systems are unstable and inefficient. Outages last quarter reach an all-time high at 8.75%.

- Secret shopper results place efficiency of customer service reps in the bottom quartile of the industry.

HOW **KEY CHANGES BEING DELIVERED**

IT Systems

- Upgrade the underlying infrastructure by installing two sets of redundant ADM servers ($1.1M)
- ADM desktop applications installed on 35 PCs ($0.1M)

Process Design

- "Seven Sigma Inc." selected through RFP to implement end-to-end process overhaul ($0.8M)
- Processes designed around ADM functionality

Training

- HR to lead training efforts based on ADM modules for 8 managers and 27 customer reps ($0.2M)

THE DRIVING FORCES

Stream	Details	Jan	Feb	Mar	Apr
IT	• Upgrade core servers • Transition to new order application	▬▬	▬▬	▬	
Process Design	• Map existing processes • Document new processes	▬▬	▬		
Training	• Training for managers • Training for customer reps			▬▬	
Launch					★

LAUNCH PLANNED FOR FIRST WEEK OF APRIL
• Leaves sufficient time for defect fixes before spring promotions scheduled in May

Framework: communicating change

Let's face it, sometimes you work with morons. It's surprising some of them get their shoelaces tied properly and make it to work on time. In order to make your life easier, you may need to convince them to start doing things a little bit differently. But if you just blurt out the obvious solution, they may not get it. So let's look at a way to lead them to the right result.

There's a handsome fellow named Robert Harris who wrote a book with the clumsy title *Change Leadership — Inform, Involve, Ignite*, which provides a pretty good approach for this. In case you want to sound really clever when you talk to people about communicating change, you can refer to the model that he uses, pictured to the right, as "strategic influencing."

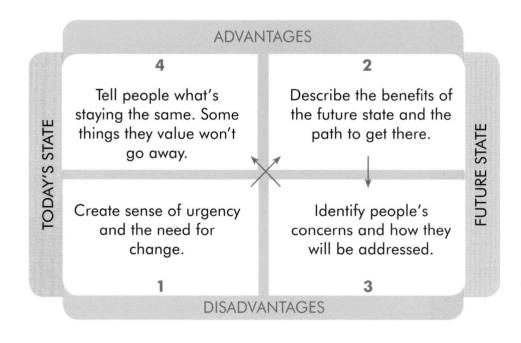

ADVANTAGES

TODAY'S STATE

FUTURE STATE

4
Tell people what's staying the same. Some things they value won't go away.

2
Describe the benefits of the future state and the path to get there.

1
Create sense of urgency and the need for change.

3
Identify people's concerns and how they will be addressed.

DISADVANTAGES

Here are the steps in this framework, summarized in the diagram above:

1. Start by creating a sense of urgency about the current state of affairs. This is often referred to as creating a "burning platform," which is a term that originated from a happy little story about a man who was faced with the choice between burning to death on a fiery oil rig or jumping into the freezing cold waters of the North Atlantic (he jumped). Your goal here is to create the sense that people need to do something right away in order to avoid a bad situation.

2. Next, you want to take people to a happy place. Paint them a picture of the flower-filled meadow that is the future state you want them to be in. Help them feel it's attainable by showing the path to get there.

3. Since some audience members may shake their canes in the air and object to any sort of change, try to anticipate and address the most common concerns people might have about the future state.

4. To ease concerns about the change, tell people that they get to bring their blankie with them. Highlight the fact that some of the things they value about the current state will still be there in the future.

Here's a quick example of this framework. It reminds any barn-raised co-workers to wash their hands after using the bathroom.

HEPATITIS

is what we'll all get if we don't
change our bathroom habits **now**.

IMAGINE

an office that is safe, clean, and free of germs. We can get this simply by **washing our hands** after using the bathroom.

DRY HANDS

will be overcome by providing
moisturizer at each sink.

DON'T WORRY,

you can still bring your
newspaper with you.

The three-act storyline

This is the granddaddy of telling a story with a slide deck, so sit up straight and show some respect. The guy who really nails how to do this is Cliff Atkinson, as he describes in his book *Beyond Bullet Points*. If you want to get deep inside this approach, go read his book. This section will give you the essentials.

Once upon a time in a land far, far away, there was a slick-talker named Aristotle, who came up with a bunch of nifty ideas. One was about the best way to tell stories, which he based on a simple three-act structure. And he must have gotten it right, since 2,400 years later this structure is still being used in plays, movies, and even TV commercials. So if it's good enough for these big-budget productions, it should be good enough for our slides.

Here's how it works:

Act 1: This provides the setting for the story, introduces the main characters, and kicks off some kind of emotional imbalance (perhaps a looming crisis or a potential opportunity) that carries throughout the rest of the story.

Act 2: This is where the bulk of the action takes place and the story unfolds. The characters work their way through the emotional imbalance that was introduced in Act 1.

Act 3: The drama and tension build to the climax, where a grand solution is revealed and all the loose ends are neatly tied up.

Whether you know it or not, this is basically how you've been hearing stories your entire life. Since we've been taking in information this way all along, let's look at how to use it in a presentation. In this example, a medical company's retail division is concerned about conflicting priorities with the wholesale division. The wholesale division wants to ease those concerns.

THE RELATIONSHIP BETWEEN WHOLESALE AND RETAIL

ACME MEDICAL CORP

Act 1

There are five things that should be covered in the first act of your story. You can have a slide for each or combine several of these on a single slide, depending on what works best for you. These five things are:

1. The setting: The time and place of the story.
2. The main character: Almost always your audience.
3. The emotional imbalance: The potential crisis or opportunity that's driving the whole story.
4. The balance: Letting your audience know that the imbalance you raised isn't the end of the world, so they don't get too scared.
5. The solution: Some foreshadowing that shows how everything will turn out all right. This is where you introduce the main points of your argument, which you will detail in Act 2.

THERE IS A RANGE OF COMPETITION IN THE US MARKET TODAY

Place — Time

Coyote Medical — TNT Instruments

Acme Wholesale — Main character

Anvil Supplies Ltd — International entrants

THE WHOLESALE DIVISION WORKS IN THE SAME MARKET

Acme Wholesale
→ TNT Instruments
→ Coyote Medical
→ Anvil Supplies Ltd
→ International entrants

The wholesale division sells to all of these competitors — Emotional imbalance

Maintaining the competitiveness of the retail division is wholesale's top priority. — Emotional balance

WHOLESALE SUPPORTS THE RETAIL STRATEGY IN THREE UNIQUE WAYS:
- Competitive intelligence
- Regulatory support
- Economic growth

Foreshadowing the solution

Act 2

This is where you put some meat on the bones and use some insights from all your years of experience. Whereas Act 1 toys with your audience's emotions, Act 2 is all business, all the time. Try to put your major points into groups of three. This will help people follow your story as well as make it a lot easier for them to remember what you talked about (see page 112 in the "How we process information" section for more detail). If you're going to be presenting in person under a time limit, Cliff Atkinson has some guidelines that can help you match the length of your slide deck to the time you have available. Here's a summary of what he says:

- If you only have 5 minutes to cover your material, use just one slide for each of your three main points in Act 2.
- If you have 15 minutes, add an additional three slides for sub-points of each of the main points you want to make.
- If you have 45 minutes, add an additional three slides for the next level of detail.

Confused? No kidding. The table below illustrates what the slide structure of Act 2 might look like if you were to follow Atkinson's guidelines (each line in the table would be a separate slide):

5 MINUTES	15 MINUTES	45 MINUTES
Point 1	Supporting point 1	Detail on Supporting point 1 Detail on Supporting point 1 Detail on Supporting point 1
	Supporting point 2	Detail on Supporting point 2 Detail on Supporting point 2 Detail on Supporting point 2
	Supporting point 3	Detail on Supporting point 3 Detail on Supporting point 3 Detail on Supporting point 3
Point 2	Supporting point 1	Detail on Supporting point 1 Detail on Supporting point 1 Detail on Supporting point 1
	Supporting point 2	Detail on Supporting point 2 Detail on Supporting point 2 Detail on Supporting point 2
	Supporting point 3	Detail on Supporting point 3 Detail on Supporting point 3 Detail on Supporting point 3
Point 3	Supporting point 1	Detail on Supporting point 1 Detail on Supporting point 1 Detail on Supporting point 1
	Supporting point 2	Detail on Supporting point 2 Detail on Supporting point 2 Detail on Supporting point 2
	Supporting point 3	Detail on Supporting point 3 Detail on Supporting point 3 Detail on Supporting point 3

This approach works as a rough guide, but it assumes that you need to fill all the time you're given and that your audience needs to know every painstaking detail you have to offer. Again, be sure you clearly understand what people need to know and don't bother wasting time by going into things that won't help them understand things better.

Using the medical company example, here are three slides that might form Act 2:

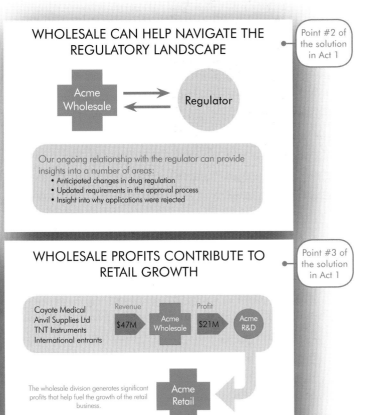

Act 3

Act 3 brings it all home and ties every-thing up with a neat little bow. Here are a handful of recommendations for this section of a presentation:

- Restate the imbalance from Act 1.
- Restate the solution.
- Bring the story to a climax.
- Provide a resolution so that people aren't left hanging.

Okay, this slide deck isn't exactly going to win an award for the best short story, but it demonstrates a decent structure for the flow of a presentation.

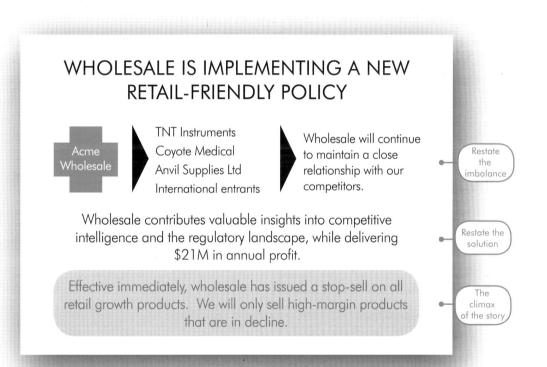

WHOLESALE AND RETAIL
WILL MAINTAIN A STRONG,
COMPLEMENTARY RELATIONSHIP.

The resolution

Those are three general ways to organize some of your thoughts into a presentation. But you can use many other frameworks, some of which are all-purpose and some of which are specific to a particular situation. The rest of this section outlines a handful of other frameworks to consider, along with examples of when each might be useful. We'll use a mix of slides that can be used for emailing and slides for use when presenting in person. Each of these frameworks can categorize your information and then structure it in a logical way.

Framework: the marketing mix

When to use it

- To explain how to differentiate a product from the competition.
- To outline a basic product strategy.

How to use it

This framework has a few variations, but the most common one is called the "4 Ps" of marketing, and it is structured around product, price, promotion, and place.

1. Product: provides an overview of the actual product or service, which often includes where it is in its life cycle (introduction, growth, maturity, saturation, decline).
2. Price: identifies how much the product is going to sell for. This often includes a comparison to competitor pricing and possibly a review of the price's elasticity (in other words, the degree to which sales volumes change when the price changes).
3. Promotion: explains how information about the product is going to be communicated to potential customers, including advertising, sales strategies, and public relations.
4. Place: describes how the product is going to be distributed.

THE MARKETING MIX:
CAT TOY SMARTPHONE APP

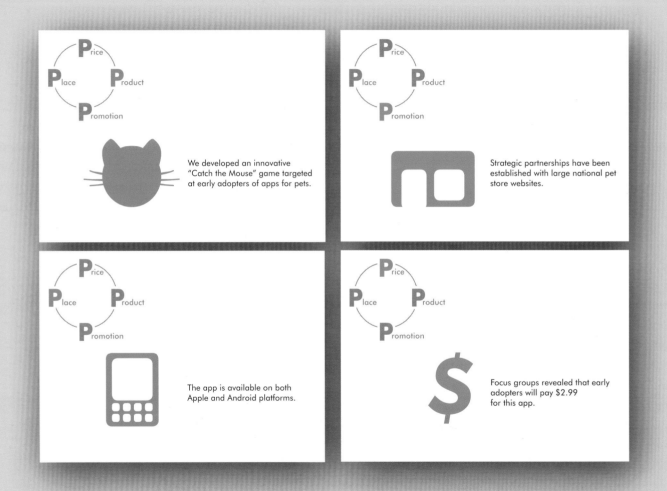

Price
Place
Product
Promotion

We developed an innovative "Catch the Mouse" game targeted at early adopters of apps for pets.

Price
Place
Product
Promotion

Strategic partnerships have been established with large national pet store websites.

Price
Place
Product
Promotion

The app is available on both Apple and Android platforms.

Price
Place
Product
Promotion

Focus groups revealed that early adopters will pay $2.99 for this app.

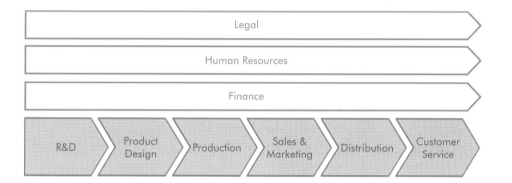

A value chain can also be used to structure a whole presentation, by looking at how a product goes through each team in the chain and detailing what they do to add value to it before it's passed to the next group (e.g., a slide or two on each of the functions in this diagram).

Framework: the value chain

When to use it

- To describe how different teams add value to a product or service.
- To show how a product flows through an organization.

How to use it

Visually, you can show a value chain in a few different ways. Sometimes it's a diagram that demonstrates how different departments fit together.

Framework: the Minto Pyramid

When to use it

- To help co-workers make a decision.
- To frame a problem and then solve it.

How to use it

A lady by the name of Barbara Minto wrote an outrageously priced book (as much as $175 at last check) about logic and problem-solving. The book outlines four steps to laying out your reasoning when you need to solve a problem or come to a decision. She refers to them as SCQA, which stands for Situation, Complication, Question, and Answer. Here's a quick overview of each:

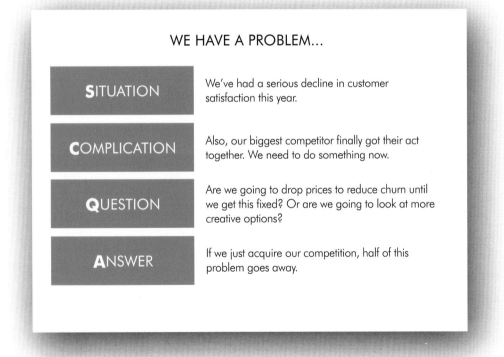

WE HAVE A PROBLEM...

SITUATION — We've had a serious decline in customer satisfaction this year.

COMPLICATION — Also, our biggest competitor finally got their act together. We need to do something now.

QUESTION — Are we going to drop prices to reduce churn until we get this fixed? Or are we going to look at more creative options?

ANSWER — If we just acquire our competition, half of this problem goes away.

Situation: describes the current or previous state. Telling people something they already know can help establish a comfortable starting point.

Complication: describes what has or is about to change. You should create a fundamental tension that begins to raise questions with the audience.

Question: spells out some of the questions that are coming up.

Answer: displays the water that you've been leading the horses to. You should make all of your major recommendations and conclusions at this step. Sometimes you will just use the first three steps as the introduction and then reveal the answer step as the main body of the presentation.

Framework: growth and development of a team

When to use it

- To demonstrate how to manage and lead a new team that has been formed to tackle a project.
- To demonstrate how to grow and develop a team of people to take on a big challenge.

How to use it

A guy by the name of Bruce Tuckman proposed that there are four basic phases that all teams go through in order to grow into high performers. If nothing else, he's given us a framework we can use to explain how to effectively develop a team:

1. **Forming:** when people initially come together on a team, they usually want to be liked and to avoid controversy. They spend time working out trivial team-interaction details, such as how often they're going to meet and who's going to take notes. They might talk about the problem and set a few objectives, but they probably won't get much else done at this phase. Whoever is in charge of these oddballs needs to use a directive management style.

2. **Storming:** the next phase is characterized by people competing to have their ideas heard. There's sometimes a debate as to what the real problems are. A bit of head-butting can occur, and not every team makes it past this phase. The leader needs to continue to be directive and provide general guidance but also allow the team to resolve some things among themselves.

3. **Norming:** during this phase, the team unites around a common goal and creates a plan for going forward.

4. **Performing:** usually, only high-performing teams make it to this phase. These teams are motivated and find a way to work together to get things done. The leader should take a participative approach and make sure the team doesn't return to an earlier phase.

OUR TEAM'S JOURNEY

- Cross-functional team came together from marketing, sales, finance, and operations
- Established basic roles and meeting schedule

FORMING...

- Intense debate about priorities
- Several workshops held with stakeholder groups

STORMING...

- Aligned on three customer service priorities
- Locked on mission statement, program timelines, and key outcomes

NORMING...

- Adapted to overcome obstacles
- Managed risks through escalations
- Delivered on time and under budget

PERFORMING...

Framework: sustainability

When to use it

- To show how your project is going to make the world a better place.

How to use it

The three Es of sustainability is a popular maxim among the do-gooders who operate in both business and non-profit circles. It explains how you can make money while doing good things for people as well as the environment, which is often referred to as the "triple bottom line." If you're looking for an approach that is most likely to see you end your presentation with a hug, try this one.

The three Es around which to build your presentation are:

1. **Economics:** this section explains the financials of your initiative.
2. **Social equity:** here you would explain how your initiative is improving the quality of people's lives, whether they are employees, customers, or members of the community.
3. **The environment:** here you would describe all of the trees and whales that you would save.

THE TRIPLE BOTTOM LINE OF OUR NEW FACTORY

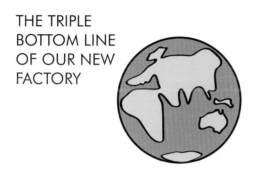

eCONOMICS

$20M in new annual revenue

eNVIRONMENT

1 ton reduction in carbon emissions

SOCIAL eQUITY

500 new jobs created in our community

Framework: decision-making

When to use it

- To walk people through the finer details of a decision-making process.

How to use it

This is a good approach to use when you need to guide people through each part of the decision-making process. There are seven basic steps you can structure your presentation around:

1. **Goal:** explain what the end goal is to keep the audience on track.
2. **Data:** collect data to give decision-makers the information they need.
3. **Alternatives:** brainstorm on the alternative solutions.
4. **Pros & cons:** list the pros and cons of each alternative.
5. **Decision:** recommend which alternative to pursue.
6. **Implementation:** take action to implement the decision.
7. **Learnings:** create a plan to extract knowledge from the action that will be taken.

The "Putting it all together" section will walk through an example of this framework.

Framework: business case

When to use it

- You need to present a new initiative to the relevant decision-makers, who require a lot of information.

How to use it

This is really flirting with becoming a full-fledged document rather than a slide presentation, but the framework might still be helpful for walking through a new business opportunity or when asking for money. The sections that might be used in a particular situation can vary widely, but here is one example:

1. Executive summary
2. Organizational overview
3. Business environment
4. Marketing plan
5. Operations
6. Financial statements

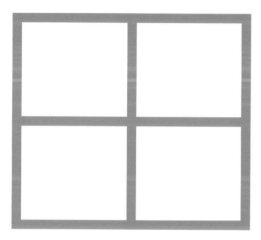

BUSINESS CASE FOR

TOMMY'S GLASS

EXECUTIVE SUMMARY

Who we are and What we do

- Family owned and operated glass installation business with eight employees
- Install high-end, custom glass for commercial and residential customers

Where we operate

- Based in Seattle, focused on the northwest of Washington State

Why we're looking for capital

- Strong reputation for delivering high-value installations has fueled growth
- $150k in capital needed for purchase of vans and payroll of new employee hires to accelerate growth trajectory

Contents

Organization overview → Business environment → Marketing plan → Operations → Financial overview

ORGANIZATION OVERVIEW

Tommy
President

- 20 years experience in glass installation
- Former manager with Seattle's largest glass installer
- First-hand experience as a journeyman installer

Jane
Office Manager

- 5 years experience in bookkeeping and accounting
- Certificate in office management

Harry
General Manager

- 10 years experience in glass installation
- 5 years experience as team manager

Installer crew

- 3 journeymen glass installers
- 2 apprentice glass installers

BUSINESS ENVIRONMENT

CUSTOMER TRENDS

ECONOMIC ENVIRONMENT

COMPETITIVE LANDSCAPE

BUSINESS ENVIRONMENT | Customer trends

CUSTOMER
TRENDS

- Growing demand for glass products in both homes and businesses in the Seattle area

- Population growth of our market expected to continue at 1% per year

- Over 6,000 new businesses opening each year

ECONOMIC
ENVIRONMENT

- GDP growth of 2.5% per year in Seattle area

- Renovation spend to exceed $6B and new construction to exceed $8B next year

- Local construction industry growing at 7% per year

BUSINESS ENVIRONMENT | Competitive landscape

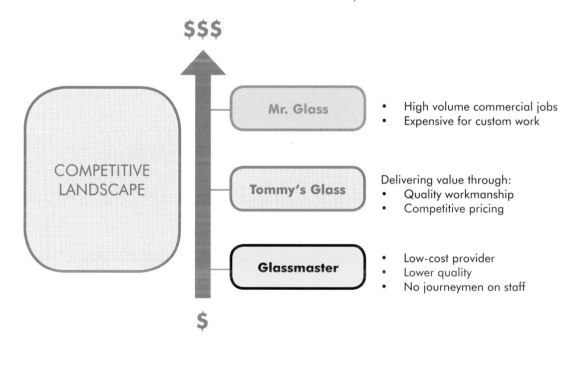

$$$

COMPETITIVE LANDSCAPE

Mr. Glass
- High volume commercial jobs
- Expensive for custom work

Tommy's Glass

Delivering value through:
- Quality workmanship
- Competitive pricing

Glassmaster
- Low-cost provider
- Lower quality
- No journeymen on staff

$

MARKETING PLAN

PRODUCT	PRICE	PROMOTION & PLACE

MARKETING PLAN

PRODUCT

Residential products include:
- Frameless showers
- Mirrors
- Backsplashes
- Hand rails
- Doors

Commercial products include:
- Storefronts
- Office interiors (partition glass, counter tops)
- Entry ways
- Business signs

MARKETING PLAN

PRICE

Residential rates:
- $50 per hour
- 25% mark-up on material
- Average job size is $750

Commercial rates:
- $75 per hour
- 25% mark-up on material
- Average job size is $2,250

MARKETING PLAN

PROMOTION
& PLACE

Strategic partnerships
- Subcontractor to the region's largest commercial installer

Designer referrals
- Partnership with five high-end interior designers

Builder contract
- Subcontractor to 10 custom home builders

$150k
$300k
$200k

Last year's revenue
- Strategic partnerships
- Designer referrals
- Builder contracts

MARKETING PLAN

Workshop:
- Centrally located workshop for prefabrication work
- Small office for records management
- Installers dispatched daily

Vehicles:
- 3 fully equipped glass installer vans
- 1 flatbed truck for oversize glass

Suppliers:
- Strong relationships with 5 majors suppliers of glass and material in the region

FINANCIAL OVERVIEW

INCOME STATEMENT

BALANCE SHEET

GROWTH PLANS

FINANCIAL OVERVIEW | Income statement

Strong year-over-year income growth

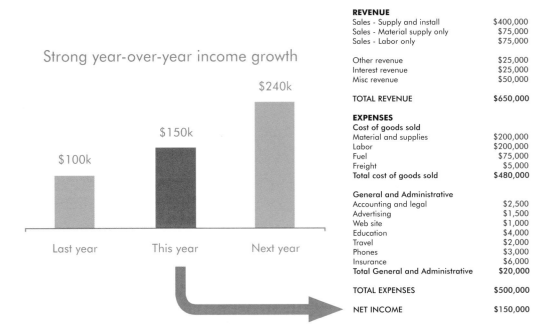

$100k — Last year
$150k — This year
$240k — Next year

REVENUE

Sales - Supply and install	$400,000
Sales - Material supply only	$75,000
Sales - Labor only	$75,000
Other revenue	$25,000
Interest revenue	$25,000
Misc revenue	$50,000
TOTAL REVENUE	**$650,000**

EXPENSES

Cost of goods sold

Material and supplies	$200,000
Labor	$200,000
Fuel	$75,000
Freight	$5,000
Total cost of goods sold	**$480,000**

General and Administrative

Accounting and legal	$2,500
Advertising	$1,500
Web site	$1,000
Education	$4,000
Travel	$2,000
Phones	$3,000
Insurance	$6,000
Total General and Administrative	**$20,000**
TOTAL EXPENSES	**$500,000**
NET INCOME	**$150,000**

FINANCIAL OVERVIEW | Balance sheet

ASSETS

Current Assets	
Cash	$20,000
Accounts receivable	$30,000
Prepaid expenses	$10,000
Total Current Assets	**$60,000**

Capital Assets	
Buildings	$430,000
Vehicles	$100,000
Office furniture	$10,000
Total Capital Assets	$540,000

TOTAL ASSETS	**$600,000**

LIABILITIES

Current liabilities	
Accounts payable	$50,000
Line of credit	$25,000
Credit cards	$25,000
Total Current Liabilities	**$100,000**

Long Term Liabilities	
Mortgage	$200,000
Loans from shareholders	$50,000
Total Long Term Liabilities	**$250,000**

EQUITY	
Share capital	$100,000
Retained earnings	$150,000
TOTAL EQUITY	**$250,000**

LIABILITIES AND EQUITY	**$600,000**

FINANCIAL OVERVIEW | Growth plans

- Revenue per installer: $130k
- Net income per installer: $30k

Growth plan: Hire 3 more installers

Buy 3 more trucks: $75,000	Installer tools & materials: $10,000	60-day payroll bridge: $65,000	Total capital needed: $150,000

$150k capital ▶ + $90k income = **60%** RETURN ON INVESTMENT

Framework: sales presentations

When to use it

- You're trying to sell someone something.

How to use it

Volumes have been written on this topic, and this book is by no means a how-to on the sales process. There really isn't a one-size-fits-all formula, since there are countless possible situations. For example, you need to take a far different approach when meeting a prospective customer for the first time than you would with a customer you've been clinking drinks with for the past 10 years. And in case you missed it the last 30 times it was pointed out, the key lies in knowing your audience by asking yourself questions about what they need from you.

That said, here is a basic framework you can follow as a starting point:

1. Company background: start by summarizing what you and your company are all about. This is a great place to list any awards or some of your best-known customers to provide a bit of third-party validation. ("Well, if all these other people like them, I guess they can't be all that bad.")

2. The customer's needs: explain what you think these are. This isn't something you necessarily need to tell them; you can frame these slides in such a way that you're asking the customer to refine your understanding of what they actually need. And because you're so quick-witted, you'll be able to tailor some of your delivery based on any refinements you uncover.

3. The solution: this is where you lay it down and show why you can meet the customer's needs. Try to be specific about what you can deliver and when you can deliver it. To make what you have to offer tangible, try to provide names, pictures, and even short bios of the people who will be delivering the solution.

4. Why you (and/or your company): explain the advantage of choosing you and why what you have to offer is far better than anything those ne'er-do-wells (your competition) have. Because you want to reinforce your credibility, this is another good place to add some third-party validation by referencing any success stories.

5. Implementation overview: now that you've explained why you're the one to go with, try to build some confidence by detailing how you're going to deliver the solution. Explain how you'll do any quality testing and how you plan to evaluate your performance.

6. Costs/price: now that it's clear you're the only one who's truly capable of pulling this off, it's time to hit them with the price. Traditional negotiation wisdom is to avoid breaking down the costs any more than absolutely necessary (if at all), but that doesn't exactly contribute to a trusting relationship. That's your call. In addition to the sticker price, you might also want to lay out the payment terms and any guarantees or warranties that come with the purchase.

7. Conclusion: This is the wrap-up, where you reiterate how you're going to deliver on what the customer needs and then outline any next steps.

If this approach works for you, feel free to forward a portion of your commission as a token of your appreciation. (However, if it doesn't work, clearly you messed it up.)

ABOUT US...

Donut Maker 3000

- 25-year history in donut-making automation
- Three-time winner of World Donut Championship
- Customers include: Fred's Pastries, Drunken Donuts, and Mermaid's Coffee

TOP CHALLENGES WITH HAND-MADE DONUTS

WHAT THE DONUT MAKER 3000 DELIVERS

Donut Maker 3000

30% lower costs than hand-made donuts

No variation in output

Production at the same level as 15 donut makers

MAKE THE SAME GREAT DONUT EVERY TIME.

WHY CHOOSE THE DONUT MAKER 3000?

INTERNATIONAL DONUT MACHINES

- Restructuring efforts have impacted R&D
- 6th place finish at World Donut Championship

PRISM DONUT MAKER

- FDA inspection into possible donut contamination

BULLSEYE DONUTS

- Unproven technology installed in only 5 locations

Donut Maker 3000

- Industry leader in donut automation
- Innovation and quality recognized at World Donut Championship
- The choice of top coffee and donut franchises

IMPLEMENTATION PLAN

	Legend
	Timeline
	Launch
	Support period

Activity	Details	Jan	Feb	Mar
Equipment installation	Donut Maker 3000 installed by trained professionals	▬		
Employee training	Employees are trained in operating and maintenance procedures	▬		
Testing and launch	One week of testing to ensure high quality donuts		▬◉	
Warranty period	Complimentary on-site support whenever needed			▬▬

Donut Maker 3000 oversees the installation and training to avoid any impact to your business.

INVESTMENT RETURNS

Donut Maker 3000

- Investment of $75,000 includes equipment, training, and warranty period
- Most customers experience a 10%–15% increase in revenue
- Donut making costs are reduced by 20%–30%

Expected return on investment

30%-45%

WHAT THE DONUT MAKER 3000 DELIVERS

 Give your customers a great donut every time.

 Lower your costs and increase your revenues.

 Let Donut Maker 3000 take care of the transition to automation.

Installation can begin within 2 weeks of contract signing.

Advanced Class

How we process information
THE RIGHT AND WRONG WAYS TO FEED A BRAIN

"The human brain starts working the moment you are born and never stops until you stand up to speak in public."
— George Jessel

Congratulations. If you've made it this far, you've passed the basic curriculum. It's time to join the advanced class with the smart kids. And what better place to start than with a study of how that big brain of yours works?

Have you ever seen a picture of a brain? It's a disgusting heap of goop. Yet it's a heap of goop that every idiot has, so you should learn a few tricks about how the brain works and how it likes to be fed.

Let's start by thinking about how you feed yourself. Pretend there is a big plate of food in front of you — food you want in your belly. If you start shoveling it down as fast as you can,

half of it is going to end up on your shirt and you might even find yourself being the lucky recipient of a Heimlich Maneuver. Your audience's brains work in a similar way, so slow down and let them take it one bite at a time.

There are three basic parts to your brain's memory function:

1. **Sensory memory:** this takes in all the sights, sounds, tastes, smells, and textures. At any given time your sensory memory is taking in a lot of information (just think of how many megapixels there would be in a digital picture of the room you're sitting in now), and most of that information stays in your memory for less than half a second before it evaporates.

2. **Short-term memory:** a very small amount of sensory information makes it through to short-term memory. Only

about five to nine things can be held there at any given time, and they stay for less than a minute. George Miller wrote a highly touted psychology paper back in 1956 called "The Magical Number Seven, Plus or Minus Two" that sums up this capacity quite nicely. You'll choke this part of your audience's brains if you try to feed them too much too fast, and it is the part you need to manage if you want people to remember what's in your presentation.

3. **Long-term memory:** this is the "belly" of the brain and where you want all of your information to end up. It holds a ton of information for years and years, as long as you can get that information through the short-term memory. If you want your audience to retain what you're saying, your goal for your slides should be to help get information into this part of the brain.

Knowing a bit about how the brain likes to be fed should shed some light on the basic presentation frameworks described in previous sections. An appropriate framework will help prevent your audience's brains from choking, as will the following suggestions:

- Minimize the amount of detail on your slides so you're not cramming too much down people's throats.
- Don't try to make people listen and read at the same time; their brains can't take it all in at once.
- Break your information into logical chunks (like we did in the "Your own little story-time" section).
- Feed people one bite at a time by making your main point and then pausing to let it soak in, or asking a question to help drive it home.

We're not going to turn this into a lesson on neuroscience, but the following advanced tips will help you design better slides:

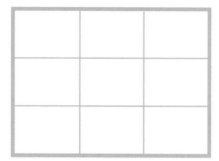

The golden ratio

For some reason, Mother Nature likes things that aren't quite square. Since the days of the Renaissance, artists, designers, and other creative types have picked up on this and have used it to their advantage. There's something called the golden rectangle, which has one side that is 1.6 times longer than the other. The brain really likes this shape. So what does this mean for you? When you want to put the brain in a good mood, start by creating a simple three-by-three grid on the slide, made up of nine rectangles like this.

The intersections where these lines cross are called power points, and they are the ideal place to position text, images, etc. This placement is more attractive and audience-friendly than a slide where everything is centered. Here's an example:

Are you going to get a standing ovation for doing this? Probably not. But anything that helps make the brain happy and more open to your message is a good thing.

This is how your eyes like to travel

Z-pattern

Typically, our eyes tend to scan a page (or screen or slide) in a particular way. So rather than trying to paddle upriver, let's recognize the current and go with the flow by placing material in the pattern that the audience naturally wants to follow.

The most common pattern is called the Z-pattern. It highlights the major points that our eyes jump to when we first see a page. The slide above shows how to place your material in the order in which people prefer to read it.

Don't underestimate the subconscious impact of putting something first. It's often perceived as being the most important point.

The rule of threes

For some reason, people tend to remember things best when they're grouped into threes, so if you can break up your material in this way, your audience is more likely to retain it. The phone companies figured out the rule of threes a long time ago. Oddly enough, few of us would be able to easily remember a number that looks like this: 8905552313. But most of us are able to cope much better with a number that looks like this: 890-555-2313.

Repetitious updates

Any time you show people a slide for the first time, a certain amount of their brainpower is spent figuring out where information is located. So if you find yourself making presentations to people regularly (e.g., a weekly project update), don't waste their precious brainpower by using a new slide format each time. Try to use the same outline and approach (or better yet, one that they're already familiar with from other projects), so that they spend a higher percentage of time on the message itself and a lower percentage of time looking for that message's location.

> *"Tell them what you're going to say, say it, tell them what you just said."*
>
> — Dale Carnegie

This is an old rule of thumb that can help your audience retain the information on your slides. Simply start by telling them what you're going to say (i.e., an agenda slide), cover all your main points (the body of your presentation), and then tell them what you just said (summary). A little repetition helps to drive the main points home.

That's it. You're not quite ready to perform brain surgery, but now you know more about your audience's brains than most of them do.

You don't stink at work
AND NEITHER SHOULD YOUR SLIDES

Seriously. Well-kept slides are right up there with brushing your teeth and cleaning your fingernails. So let's look at some basic hygiene for your slides.

Fonts

Being sloppy with your fonts is a surefire way to let everyone know that they're attending amateur hour. Follow these suggestions to avoid looking unprofessional:

- Use the same font style throughout. For example, don't use Times New Roman for one part of your slide and then `Courier` for another. It just looks shoddy.
- Don't have a rainbow of color when it comes to your fonts. Use one color, maybe two, tops. Any more than that is a distraction.

Grammar: The difference between knowing your crap and knowing you're crap.

If you didn't understand the sentence above, you're in trouble. You have to make sure your slides don't have basic grammatical errors or you're just going to lose credibility as an adult.

This section doesn't provide a comprehensive grammar review by any means. We're just going to point out a few of the common mistakes you should avoid. If you want a more complete brush-up on grammar basics without having to read something that makes you want to jump out the window, then check out a little book called *Eats, Shoots & Leaves* by Lynne Truss, which is an entirely tolerable read.

There, their, and they're

Surely you know when you're supposed to use each of these, so don't mess them up. But just in case, here's a quick summary:

There: when referring to a place ("the car is over there")

Their: used to show possession of something ("it's their car")

They're: used in place of "they are" ("they're in the car")

Your and you're

Another one that's pretty simple to keep straight:

Your: used to show possession ("your presentation will be great")

You're: a contraction used in the place of "you are" ("you're a master of the slide deck")

Who's and whose

The easiest way to make sure you're using these correctly is to get rid of the apostrophe for a second. The word "who's" is a contraction of "who is" or "who has." So if using "who is" doesn't make sense, then it's probably the right call to use "whose" instead. (Compare "who's in that office" to "whose coat is this".)

It's and its

Just as with "who's," if it's okay to use "it is" or "it has," then you can use "it's." Otherwise you should go with "its" (the possessive pronoun). This is a common one to get wrong because "its" is one of the only possessives that doesn't use an apostrophe (for example, "why would a groundhog be scared of its own shadow?").

Affect and effect

The simple difference here is that "affect" is a verb and "effect" is a noun: "Your crappy slides affect the way people feel about you. Being seen as competent is the effect you're going for."

Lead and led

This is a really common mistake. "Lead" is the present tense and "led" is the past tense, so please don't get caught saying you "lead your team yesterday."

Having someone else review your slides is a good way to catch these grammatical mishaps.

Bullet points

Bullet points make an appearance on just about every slide presentation, and all too often there are inconsistencies that distract the audience. Here is an example:

REASONS WE NEED TO ACT NOW:

- Lagging in customer satisfaction

- aggressive, competitive pressure

- We only have a few weeks before the end of the quarter.

The problem here is that every bullet point has a different format:

- One starts with a verb, another with an adjective, and another with a pronoun.
- Two begin with capital letters and one with a lower-case letter.
- One ends with a period and two do not.

It doesn't really matter which approach you use; just make sure each bullet has the same format.

English class is now over. It's time to grab your crayons and head to art class.

Coloring outside the lines

THE PSYCHOLOGY OF COLORS

This one might not seem like a big deal at first but you're getting to be so clever that we can afford to invest a bit of time in some of the finer details.

That said, the colors your company uses as part of its corporate branding and identity certainly aren't trivial. It's easy to think of a number of examples of things that are commonly referred to by their color:

Big Blue = IBM
Green Monster = left-field wall at Fenway Park
Red, White, and Blue = the USA

A company's brand is often a highly valued and much-adored asset, so don't go defiling it by misusing its colors. For example, if your company's main color is blue, then don't just pick any old blue for the diagrams you use. Rather, take a minute to get it right. The brand offices at a lot of companies can share the exact RGB (red-green-blue) composition of their brand's colors. If you have the RGB composition, you can choose the colors for line, text, and fill with precision by going to the "More Fill Colors . . ." option in PowerPoint® presentation software.

Be sure to use an equal amount of caution with the colors your main competitors use. There are emotional undercurrents that can run deeply when it comes to the competition, so be aware of how you're using colors that are associated with them. For example, don't use your competitor's shading on the text box that highlights the big deliverable by your team.

But what about when you're a free-range chicken who can choose whatever colors you like? Let's look at a couple of basic tips to help guide you: the color wheel and the psychology of colors.

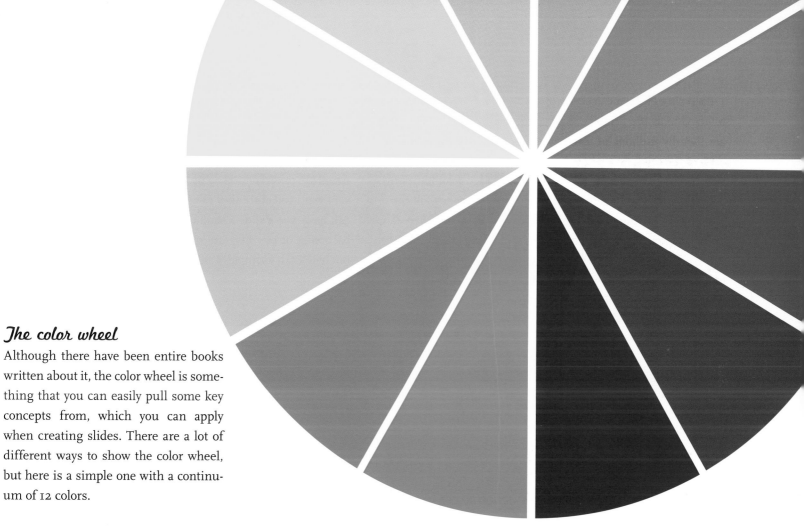

The color wheel

Although there have been entire books written about it, the color wheel is something that you can easily pull some key concepts from, which you can apply when creating slides. There are a lot of different ways to show the color wheel, but here is a simple one with a continuum of 12 colors.

Each slice of the pie is created with a combination of what are referred to as the primary colors (red, yellow, and blue). There are literally millions of different shades and hues in between each of the ones shown above, but we'll use this wheel to illustrate a couple of concepts related to what's called color harmony.

Colors can work together harmoniously when they are complementary. Using two complementary colors together can create a vibrant look and help make something stand out. But use complementary colors carefully, since they can be visually overwhelming. Complementary colors are opposite from one another on the color wheel, for example:

Don't believe these colors work together in a complementary way? Try telling Santa Claus that his favorite Christmas colors don't go together.

On the other hand, colors that are beside each other on the wheel are referred to as being analogous. They match each other very well, and since they're often found together in nature, they can help give a slide a serene, comfortable feel. Again, between each slice of pie there are millions of hues that could be used, but here is an example of three analogous colors from our wheel:

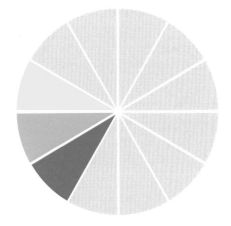

Although PowerPoint® presentation software uses a hexagonal layout, it's pretty easy to apply the color wheel using the "More Fill Colors . . ." menu. Colors that are beside each other (either in a clockwise or counterclockwise direction) are analogous, just like in the color wheel above. The colors closer to the center of the hexagon have more white in them, creating a lighter tint. Colors that are closer to the outside of the hexagon have more black, making them a darker shade. And, just like the color wheel, the complementary colors are opposite each other. The next page shows an example that uses different tints of blue combined with a complementary yellow, which helps create a contrast to highlight the main point.

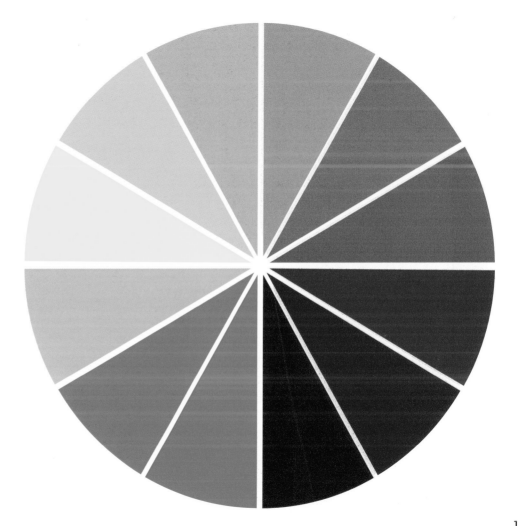

QUALITY ASSURANCE IS NEEDED BEFORE PRODUCTION STARTS

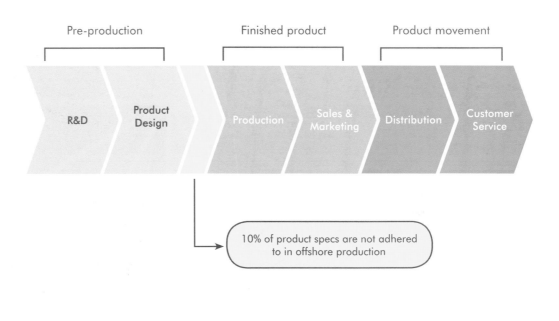

Pre-production

Finished product

Product movement

R&D

Product Design

Production

Sales & Marketing

Distribution

Customer Service

10% of product specs are not adhered to in offshore production

There are many other ways to combine colors harmoniously. Several combinations are summarized below, including what effect each can provide on a slide:

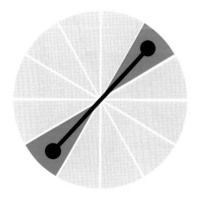

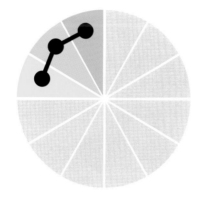

Complementary

Where found: Opposite each other

When to use / feeling expressed: Shows a contrast

Analogous

Where found: Beside each other

When to use / feeling expressed: Harmonious, comforting, natural

Triad

Where found: Three colors, equally spaced

When to use / feeling expressed: Vibrant, let one dominate, use the others for contrast

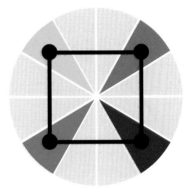

Split Complementary
Where found: Uses colors on either side of the complementary color

When to use / feeling expressed: Shows a contrast, with less tension than with complimentary

Tetradic
Where found: Two sets of complementary colors

When to use / feeling expressed: Rich color combinations, let one dominate and the others accent

Square
Where found: Four colors, equally spaced

When to use / feeling expressed: Maximum contrast between four colors, let one dominate and the others accent

> *"People can have the Model J in any color they want, just as long as it's black."*
> — Henry Ford

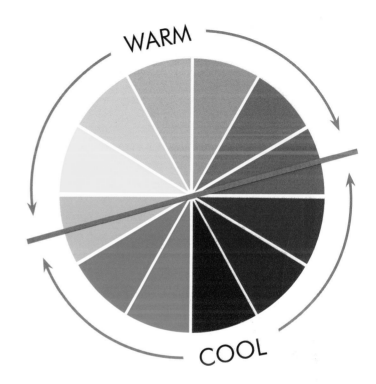

The psychology of colors

Please gather round, hold hands and get ready to talk about your emotions. At the most basic level, some colors tend to be "warm" while other colors tend to be "cool." Warm colors help to communicate energy and boldness, whereas cool colors help to communicate calmness and serenity.

Within these two broad categories, the individual colors you decide to use can subtly influence your audience's emotions and perceptions. Here is a bit of insight into the main ones.

Black is obviously the most common choice for text because it provides the greatest contrast to a white background. In the world of business, black numbers typically mean that they're positive (greater than zero) or that there has been a profit ("we're in the black!").

Because it's so common, black doesn't convey a lot of emotion. But it can be used in images or backgrounds to subtly evoke quite a few different feelings. For example:

- Darkness and evil (heavy metal bands)
- Formality and sophistication (the little black dress)
- Power and authority (a tuxedo . . . or a ninja)
- Mystery and emptiness (space)

White is a great background color because so many other colors stand out well against it. But white can also convey different emotions, such as:

- Peacefulness (a cloud or a white flag)
- Purity (virgin snow)
- Safety and security (a white picket fence)
- Cleanliness (doctors and nurses)
- Openness and new beginnings

> *"I told my dentist my teeth are going yellow. He told me to wear a brown tie."*
>
> — Rodney Dangerfield

> *"It's not easy being green."*
>
> — Kermit the Frog

Apparently, yellow is the happiest color. Unfortunately, a guy by the name of Harvey Ball (no relation to the Harvey Balls introduced earlier, but that's a weird coincidence) discovered this back in the 1960s when he created that smug yellow smiley face logo that continues to plague society.

The happy feelings that yellow can evoke tend to contradict two of the most common uses we have for it:

- Status: "Caution, all is not well."
- Traffic lights: "Floor it, we need to get through before it turns red."

Nevertheless, using different shades of yellow in imagery is a good way to send positive vibes to your audience, giving them a sense of optimism and happiness.

For some reason people love green. It's the favorite color of both capitalists and environmentalists, and they don't agree on a heck of a lot.

When you're on dry land, green is the most abundant color in the world, so it's one that people are usually comfortable with. Common associations with the color green include:

- Tranquility and harmony (nature)
- Growth and renewal (again, nature)
- Prosperity (money)

Between the sky and the ocean, the color blue is everywhere. No wonder it ranks as people's favorite color (that is, according to wiki.answers.com, and the Internet is never wrong). In general practice, the color blue is associated with a lot of different things (baby boys, first-place ribbons, depression), but outside of these day-to-day uses, some of the emotions that different shades of blue evoke include:

- Deep blue: calmness and serenity (a calm ocean)
- Soft blue: ice and cold (a frozen lake)
- Bright blue: energy and vigor (Superman's outfit)

Does the color red really make bulls mad? Maybe. If only humans were so simple, and we only had one reaction to red. The color red's most common use in business is to show a loss (versus a profit) or to show that a particular number is negative (less than zero). On the soft and fluffy side, people may experience many different feelings when they see this color, including:

- Stimulation (lipstick, sports cars, red tag sales)
- Increased energy and heart rate (must be what that bull feels)
- Confidence (a red necktie)

> *"Roses are red, violets are blue. Poor violet, violated for a rhyme."*
>
> — Derek Jarman

> *"People do give me a hard time about my hair because it's orange and it's big."*
>
> — Carrot Top

Barney notwithstanding, purple is a color that is generally associated with royalty and valor. It's a combination of both red and blue and tends to find a balance between the stimulation and calmness that those colors provide. Some of the emotions linked to purple include:

- Calmness and serenity (lavender)
- Bravery (the Purple Heart)

Who knew that we had a bad boy in our midst? Apparently orange is the most controversial color, dividing people between the "love it" and "hate it" camps. It should be used with caution, but it does evoke two emotions:

- Stimulation or a call to action (the sun)
- Appetite (pumpkin pie)

> ## *"Picasso had his pink period and his blue period. I am in my blonde period right now."*
>
> — Hugh Hefner

That should be all you need to know about choosing colors for your slides. Hopefully this newly acquired knowledge won't leave you dumbstruck the next time you get dressed for work, imagining all the subtle things your clothes are telling people.

Pink is in the midst of a bit of a makeover. Traditionally associated with all things young and girly, it's also been the campaign color behind things like breast cancer awareness and anti-bullying. Go, pink, go.

Outside of the good old pink slip, it's not a color that's used a heck of a lot in the business world, but if it's something that works for your presentation, here are a few of the feelings linked to it:

- Youthfulness, fun, excitement (Barbie)
- Romance (flowers)

Cranking up your sass factor

WITH TABLES, GRAPHS, AND DIAGRAMS

That's right, time to sass things up by taking your data to the next level. Have you ever sat through a presentation that is nothing but bullet points of facts and data? Did you stay awake for it? It's a really lousy way to present information. This section walks you through an example of a complete data makeover. Consider it "Extreme Makeover Presentation Edition."

Let's start with an example of a dreadful list of bullet points describing the performance of a national sales team:

- Southern California suffered from the impact of a recent heat wave that resulted in actual sales that were $500k under target for the month.
- We hired 4 more people in Oregon, which contributed to our best month ever in the state. Total sales were $4.3M which was $400k over target!
- Team Nevada definitely did not hit the jackpot. Last month's sales performance missed the target by over 30%.
- The Washington area is generally benefiting from strong cross-border growth, with last month's sales coming in at $200k over target.

One step up the evolutionary chain from bullet points is a table. The benefit of a table is that it pushes the data toward consistent units of measure (i.e., each column uses the same kind of data), so readers can scan through the rows until they find what they want to focus on. But you're still asking people to sift through a lot of data to find whatever it is they need to know, with the rest of the detail being far less relevant or perhaps even completely useless.

STATE OR TERRITORY	TARGET ($M)	ACTUAL ($M)	VARIANCE ($)	VARIANCE (%)
Alabama	$4.8	$4.7	-$0.1	-2.1%
Alaska	$0.7	$0.7	-$0.0	-3.1%
Arizona	$6.5	$6.4	-$0.1	-1.3%
Arkansas	$2.9	$3.1	$0.2	5.5%
California	$37.7	$37.2	-$0.5	-1.3%
Colorado	$5.1	$5.3	$0.2	3.6%
Connecticut	$3.6	$3.4	-$0.2	-5.0%
Delaware	$0.9	$0.9	$0.0	0.3%
Florida	$19.1	$20.0	$0.9	4.9%
Georgia	$9.8	$10.1	$0.3	2.9%
Hawaii	$1.4	$1.2	-$0.2	-12.7%

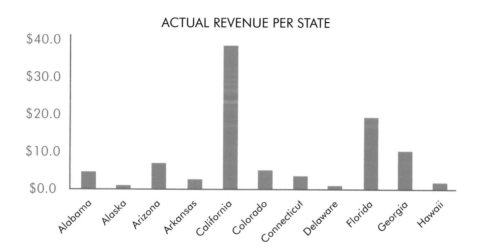

ACTUAL REVENUE PER STATE

The simplest way to improve on a table is a graph. Graphs allow people to understand a few key messages in seconds. For example, with the graph above, your eyes are immediately drawn to the tallest bars, which represent the states with the highest sales revenues. Sometimes a slide (particularly one made for an emailed presentation) will have both a graph and a table of data. The graph helps to convey a few key messages, and the table allows people to get more detail on their own.

But there are many different kinds of graphs in the world, and you need to know when to use the right one. And so, even though this is a book about PowerPoint® slides, you're getting some bonus material on Excel graphs for no extra charge.

Here are some basic guidelines on when to use each of the most common types of graphs:

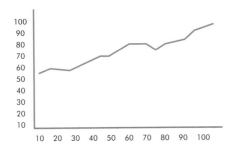

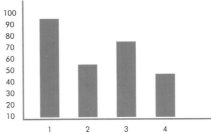

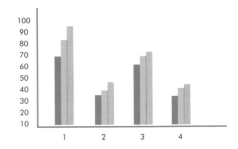

BASIC LINE GRAPH

- This is most often used to show a trend.
- The horizontal axis should be continuous (e.g., time, number of employees, etc.).

BASIC BAR GRAPH

- This is most often used to show differences between distinct categories.

CLUSTERED BAR GRAPH

- Brings an element of change (usually time) to show what's happening in different categories.

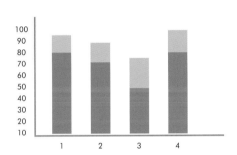

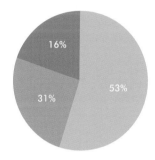

STACKED BAR GRAPH

- Shows a "before and after" view, or the impact that something will have by adding it.

PIE GRAPH

- Useful when the things you're talking about add up to 100% of the picture.

MONTHLY SALES PERFORMANCE
RELATIVE TO TARGET

-$0.6M
-$0.4M
-$0.3M
-$0.8M
-$0.5M
$1.1M

☐ Within 5% of target
■ More than 10% below target
▨ More than 10% above target
$ Magnitude of variance

But even as pretty as some of these look, a graph isn't always the most compelling way to make a point visually. Key messages don't always jump off the page.

The epitome of presenting data is getting it into a diagram. I'm not going to blow smoke by saying this is easy to do or that it's even possible to do in every situation, but using diagrams will help take your visuals from good to great.

Oh, yeah. The image to the left is a thing of beauty. Just compare it to the table on page 134 and the graph on page 135, which contain the same data, to see the difference in the impact. At one glance, people can see where things are going great (green) and where some ass-kicking is in order (red). At second glance, people can see to what extent each market needs attention (the $ figures). All the other data, which isn't relevant (i.e., states whose revenue is on target), doesn't distract from the stuff that needs to be discussed. Want to see some other examples of great visual representations of data? Check out www.powerthroughpresentations.com.

A few tips of the trade

You're starting to get an idea of what makes a slide pretty and what makes a slide ugly. Now let's look at how to make the most of a couple of time-savers that are built right into the PowerPoint® software so that you can work like a pro.

Format Painter

The Format Painter lets you transfer all of the attributes of one object (border thickness, font style, fill color) onto another object so that they have the same look and feel. This can be done in three easy steps:

1. Select the object that has the style you want to copy.
2. Click Format Painter on the menu bar.
3. Select the object you want the formatting copied to.

Aligning

When you want a bunch of objects on the slide to snap to attention and get into single file, simply use the Align tool.

There are a total of eight different alignment options you can choose from, and we'll look at a few examples here. Regardless of which you choose, the steps are pretty simple:

1. Select the objects you want to align.
2. Click the Drawing Tools tab, then click the Align drop-down menu.
3. Select whichever alignment option you want from the menu items.

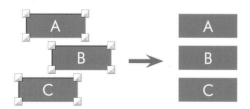

The other slick option is to click either Distribute Horizontally or Distribute Vertically (found in the Align menu), which will make all of the objects you select equally spaced (between the two outermost objects). Here's an example of what Distribute Vertically does:

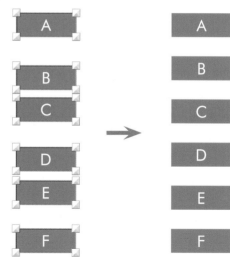

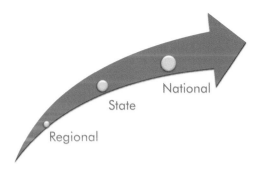

Regional / State / National

LAUNCH
• Product launch planned for April 1

LEARN
• Feedback group established to gain insights

ADJUST
• Product team will revise as necessary

SmartArt

Want to feel like a graphic designer without having to go out and purchase dark-rimmed glasses and a tight-fitting cardigan? The SmartArt® feature in PowerPoint® software is a really easy way to make your slides go from geek to chic in a couple of clicks. Just go to the Insert menu, click on SmartArt, and out pops a genie from the bottle, ready to grant you some graphical wishes.

There are tons of great graphics ready for you to use. All you have to do is select the one you want, add some text, and you're off to the races. Spend some time playing around with this feature so you can understand how best to take advantage of it. Here are just a couple of examples of the kinds of customizable graphics available in SmartArt®.

OUR BUSINESS UNIT

Legal

HR

Comms

Brand

MARKETING

Product development

Consumer

Business

Finish Line

STILL READING? OKAY,

Let's put it all together now

Is your head starting to swell with all these new insights that will help you become a presentation superhero? Good. Now we're going to walk through an example that pulls a bunch of concepts together and puts them into action. This sample presentation combines tips and tricks for creating great-looking individual slides and for laying out those slides within a logical framework, so you can create an effective slide deck.

Let's start with a little role playing. (No, not that kind of role playing.) Let's pretend you've been thrown into the deep end of a project, and you need to swim your way out using a flashy slide deck. Here's a little bit about the situation:

Your company
Make-Believe Railway Inc.

Your role
You're a project manager supporting a major expansion of a railway line.

The situation
Your boss just got transferred to a different department because he wasn't able to effectively communicate what was going on with the expansion, and the leadership team felt he was to blame for some recent setbacks.

You've been working on this project for years, and you know everything there is to know about the expansion, including the potential troubles spots and what will happen if the project goes off the rails. (Yes, that was a lame pun.)

The project is severely behind schedule, which your dearly departed boss failed to address. In order to get things where they need to be, your company is going to have to either spend more money to add additional construction crews or lower the quality of the railway construction. And if neither of these options is appealing, everyone can just keep doing what your old boss was doing and miss the original timeline. But since making this kind of decision is well above your pay grade, you need to involve the high-priced help you're presenting to.

The meeting

The meeting will be attended by a number of the company's senior leaders, including your new boss (the VP of Project Management) and his boss, the Chief Operating Officer. Both the VP of Finance and the VP of Sales will also be there.

You've been asked to present to them in person, and you know that they're also going to email your slides to other people on their teams. In order to really impress people, you've decided to create two separate decks.

So that's the situation. You have to step in for your old boss and not only update these people on what's going on but get them to make a pretty big decision so you can lead the project effectively.

What's the first thing you're going to do? If you said anything other than "understand what the audience needs," then shame on you, please go back and start reading this book again from the beginning.

The best way to figure out what people need to know is by asking them directly (surprise, surprise). If you're able to do that with any of these decision-makers (e.g., your new boss), by all means, take advantage of it. In this particular situation, you won't be able to speak to everyone, though, given how hectic their calendars are and the fact that you've never even met some of them. So you're going to ask your peers, friends at work (if applicable), and perhaps people who work for each of these leaders what this group will need to get out of your presentation. The more you refine your focus, the more effective your presentation will be. Let's not blow the dust off the analogy of building a strong foundation for your house to reinforce this point.

Let's say that after your "shaking hands and kissing babies" tour, you come up with the following insights into why each person cares about this project:

VP of Project Management (your new boss)

- He has the VP-level accountability for delivering the project on time and on budget. Part of his performance bonus is likely tied to the expansion project.
- He has a bit of egg on his face because of your old boss. He needs to try to recover by having people feel like they can have confidence in you.
- When measuring his success at the end of the year, the highest weightings will be for things like program delivery (timing), program spending (capital), and program throughput (total number of programs his team delivers).
- He is also accountable for eight other major programs. If he assigns more money or people to the expansion, he risks having some of his other projects miss their objectives.

Chief Operating Officer (your boss's boss)

- She shares all of the VP of Project Management's interests, although to a somewhat lesser extent given that she has a wider scope of accountability.
- She is taking into account one of the company's top corporate priorities, increasing its access to Asian markets, which this program is critical to.
- She is also accountable for all of the purchasing and procurement functions within the company and needs to control external spending.

VP of Finance

- He needs to understand how major projects could affect corporate financials.

- He also has concerns over meeting this year's profit targets.
- Because of delays and deferrals in other projects, the company is spending less capital than planned. This means that opportunities to capitalize any expenditure that would otherwise be opex (operational expenses) could help the profitability challenge.

VP of Sales

- The sales team has been speaking to customers for years about the rail expansion, and many customers have planned parts of their business around it. The VP of sales does not want to see any delays.

You've been on this project for years, and you know everything there is to know about it. You know that:

- the data center needs additional servers so it can handle the increased signaling data for the track sensors;
- there are three outstanding permits that are needed to complete construction in Oregon;
- there is the risk of a labor stoppage with the track-layers' union;
- the vendor you're using for one of the specialized railway tools had a disruption in its overseas factory.

So what should you include in your presentation? Here are three questions to ask yourself when deciding what to leave in and what to take out:

1. Does this information help address something the audience cares about?
2. Does it inform the audience's decision-making process? (In this case, you need to get a decision on what to do about being behind schedule. The answer to this question will inform a lot of that other stuff.)
3. Is there anything that the audience doesn't know that would be critical to their decision-making?

It takes a fair amount of effort to decide what information to put on your slides. And once you manage to get through that, you still need to figure out how to whip it all into pretty visuals, and then you need to settle on an order to lay it out. That's a lot of figuring out. Good thing you're on your way to becoming a presentation wizard.

So let's look at what to include and how to lay it out. Spend some time doing things the old-fashioned way, by pulling out a pencil and paper. People have been brainstorming this way for ages, so it might be something that helps you, too. Or perhaps you're into feeling like a professor and prefer a whiteboard and markers. Either way, start by scribbling down the main points your audience needs you to cover (which we did earlier in this section for each audience member). Then group these points into a few common themes. Here's an example of how you might categorize some of your key points about the Make-Believe Railway expansion:

- He has the VP-level accountability for delivering this on time and on budget. Part of his performance bonus is likely pegged to the expansion project.
- On his team's scorecard for how he measures his success, the highest weightings are for things like program delivery (timing), program spending (capital), and program throughput (total number of programs his team delivers).

PROJECT PERFORMANCE

- He is also accountable for eight other major programs. If the expansion needs more money or people, it's going to put his other projects at risk of missing their objectives.
- Because of delays and deferrals in other projects, the company is spending less capital than planned. This means that opportunities to capitalize any expenditures that would otherwise be opex could help the profitability challenge.

RELATIONSHIP TO OTHER PROJECTS

- The VP of Finance is there because she needs to understand how major projects could impact corporate financials
- Some of your conversations with people around the office have helped you understand that there is pressure to meet this year's profits
- She also has accountability for all of the purchasing and procurement functions within the company and needs to control external spend.

FINANCIALS

- The sales team members have been speaking to customers for years about the rail expansion. Many customers have planned parts of their business around this. The VP of Sales does not want to see any delays.
- One of the top corporate priorities is increasing the company's access to Asian markets, which this program is critical to.

CUSTOMERS

The simple act of grouping these points into categories will help you to begin organizing your thoughts. And now that you have key points in front of you, let's choose a framework for the story and then pull together a quick storyboard.

Since we need this group to make a decision, let's use the "decision-making" framework (outlined on page 84) as the template. And since we are fortunate enough to have the gift of independent thought, we're not going to follow the template exactly. Rather, we're going to use it as a guide and adapt it as much as we need.

From the previous section, here's the outline for the decision-making storyline:

1. **Goal:** explain what the end goal is to keep the audience on track.
2. **Data:** collect data to give decision-makers the information they need.
3. **Alternatives:** brainstorm on the alternative solutions.
4. **Pros & cons:** list the pros and cons of each alternative.
5. **Decision:** recommend which alternative to pursue.
6. **Implement:** take action to implement the decision.
7. **Learn:** plan for extracting learning from the action that will be taken.

We're going to begin storyboarding by putting the titles down for each slide. If we happen to have some content, we'll throw it in as a placeholder, but otherwise we're just trying to establish how the story will flow. Don't expect the end product to follow these titles exactly. Rather, we're creating something that can be discussed, debated, and changed. Once you've established the flow of your presentation, you can then build out the details for both the emailing slides and the in-person slides. Here goes:

GOAL: MAKE A DECISION ON THE EXPANSION'S NEXT STEPS

DATA: THERE ARE KEY DATA POINTS WE ALL SHOULD KNOW

ALTERNATIVES: WE HAVE THREE CHOICES

- Do nothing
- Hire more crews
- Lower the quality

PROS & CONS: THERE ARE DIFFERENT IMPACTS FOR EACH

- Do nothing: we'll miss our schedule, but probably come in on budget
- Hire more crews: meet the schedule, blow the budget
- Lower quality: meet the schedule & budget, but add risk to future operations

DECISION: RECOMMENDATION

- Do nothing
- Hire more crews
- Lower the quality

IMPLEMENTATION: HERE'S THE PLAN...

LEARN: NEXT STEPS /
PLANS TO FOLLOW-UP

MAKE-BELIEVE RAILWAY INC.

STATUS REVIEW OF THE EXPANSION PROJECT

Your name
Date

So how long do you think it would take you to throw something like this together? If your answer is greater than 10 minutes, you need to start using more than just your index fingers when you're typing.

Now, review the deck with other people to get their thoughts. It's better to get input early and often in order to minimize the amount of time you waste creating beautiful slides that you end up tossing. This is also the time to reorder your material and add or remove content.

So let's say that you find some people who are smarter than you are (as difficult as that might be to imagine), and after reviewing the slides with them, you end up with a couple of good suggestions:

- The people you're presenting to usually like to see a detailed agenda slide at the beginning.
- They also like to have an overview slide that outlines where the projects are at.

Being the thoroughbred racehorse that you are, you're probably chomping at the bit, eagerly wanting to create some slides. And since it's very likely you'll be sending this to people, let's start with the title page for the emailing presentation:

There are a few things worth considering for this slide. The first thing is the colors. The Make-Believe Railway Company uses gray and green in its brand, so we'll want to make sure the rest of the deck is consistent with this color scheme. And the company doesn't use just any old gray or green, but the ones used here. If you already have a slide or two from the company, it's easy to make the colors consistent. Use the Format Painter tool to copy styles from one object in a PowerPoint® slide to another. And if there's a competitor whose brand prominently features another color (blue, for example), then we're going to be extra cautious about how we use that color, perhaps avoiding it altogether.

Also note that on this slide, we've aligned the graphics and the text with the "power points" on the page.

This alignment is only subtly different from centering everything on the slide, but it does a couple of things:

- It improves the aesthetics by positioning things in a way that the brain naturally prefers.
- It gives a sense of room for movement and growth by positioning the train on the left-hand side of the slide (which is kind of what your project is about).

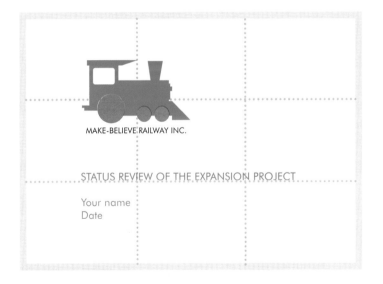

MAKE-BELIEVE RAILWAY INC.

STATUS REVIEW OF THE EXPANSION PROJECT

Your name
Date

Are little things like these going to make or break your presentation? Of course not. However, paying attention to these details will help you put people in a better mental space (even if only by a little bit), and you'll come off as a more polished and refined presenter, increasing the confidence that people have in you and what you're talking about.

Now that we have a title slide, let's take the plunge into the first slide of the presentation. There are a couple of things that we know we should try to do, right from the start:

1. State that you're here because you need this group to make a decision.

2. Lead the audience on the journey you want them to take (in other words, the agenda for the slide presentation).

Here's a simple slide you could start with:

WHY ARE WE HERE TODAY?

OUTCOME:
Make a decision on the next steps for the expansion project that takes into account impacts to:
• Customers
• Project timelines
• Financials
• Impact to other projects

AGENDA FOR TODAY
• Project overview
• Analysis of the current status
• Alternatives for next steps
• Pros & cons of the alternatives
• Recommended course of action
• Implementation plan
• Follow-up

What does this slide do? First off, it tells people what you want them to walk away from the presentation with: a decision. Also, because you did your homework, you know what's important to these people, and you've listed the major categories that you came up with earlier (customers, project timelines, financials, and impact on other projects). This tells your audience that you plan to cover things that are important to them. And finally, by including the agenda, you are showing them the path that you plan to take during the presentation. This will give them a sense of how each slide fits together and where you're heading. And if someone is reading this slide in the cold, dark confines of the cubicle farm, they're going to understand what the rest of the slides are there to do.

Luckily, one of the smart kids you spoke with during your storyboarding told you that this audience likes to have an overview slide early on, so let's create one of those. We're also going to borrow a page from the three-act framework and use this slide as an opportunity to set up some kind of an emotional imbalance in order to grab the audience's attention. Here's an example.

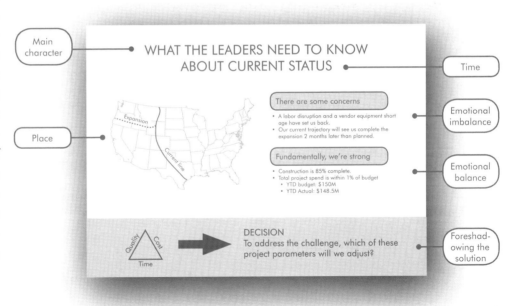

Before any of these people can make a decision, they're going to need to understand the situation in more detail. To help them, let's lay out some of the key facts and data that will inform their decision.

Hath thou ever laid eyes on a more beautiful slide? Yes, of course you have, this looks like something you'd light on fire and leave on your neighbor's doorstep. But this slide might be useful in the emailing version of your deck, for those who will be reading your presentation by themselves. It's certainly not something you'd ever put onscreen if you're in the room or on the phone presenting.

KEY DATA POINTS TO KNOW FOR THIS DECISION

Current schedule delay
- Original completion date was October 20
- 2-month delay puts projected completion date at December 20
- Impact: We would miss the holiday shipping season (worth $2M)

Labor options
- Labor disruption with track layers' union now resolved
- Extra crews can be hired at $100k / week
  - Each additional crew shortens timeline by 1 week
  - Maximum is four additional crews; no additional time savings would be realized with a fifth crew

Quality
- A lower-quality rail material can be used, saving $3M in construction costs
- Lower quality rail is expected to require up to $500k in additional annual maintenance
- Construction timelines could be improved by up to 1 month

Scope options
- Track sensors are costing $750k and are adding four weeks to the critical path
  - Not adding them would introduce significant operational risk
- While building new track, we could also lay fiber optic cable to sell to telecoms
  - Additional $2M in project costs, additional two months to complete

KEY DATA POINTS TO KNOW FOR THIS DECISION

Fiber optic cable
- $2M
- 2 months

Current schedule delay
- $2M
- 2 months

Labor options
- $400K
- 1 month

Delay track sensors
- $750k
- 1 month

Lower quality
- $2M capex
- 1 month

Impact on project cost

Impact on timelines

We'll look at the in-person slide deck in more detail later in this section, but let's pause for a minute and think about how can we get this information into a format that's easy on the eyes and better to speak to in person. Start by considering what these four categories have in common: time and money. For some reason, senior leaders love charts and graphs, so let's use the time and money parameters to create something they'll like. Here's an example of what we might create as an in-person alternative to the "reading" slide above.

If you like, you can even create slides so that each of these five bubbles appear on the screen at different times, allowing you to focus the discussion on one point at a time.

Let's check where we're at with this story. Here's what we've done so far:

1. Explained why we're here (to make a decision on the expansion).
2. Provided an overview (to get everyone on the same page).
3. Created an imbalance or burning platform (see page 63), then set up a balance and foreshadowed the solution.
4. Shared some data that will inform the decision.

Next, we're going to lay out a few possible courses of action. In some cases, you might want to describe the alternatives and then have the audience decide which route to take. In our case, since you're such an expert on the expansion, we're going to lay out the alternatives and then recommend a course of action.

Here's what this slide might look like:

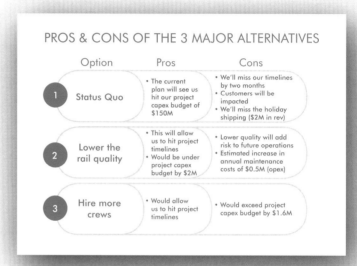

PROS & CONS OF THE 3 MAJOR ALTERNATIVES

Option	Pros	Cons
1 Status Quo	• The current plan will see us hit our project capex budget of $150M	• We'll miss our timelines by two months • Customers will be impacted • We'll miss the holiday shipping ($2M in rev)
2 Lower the rail quality	• This will allow us to hit project timelines • Would be under project capex budget by $2M	• Lower quality will add risk to future operations • Estimated increase in annual maintenance costs of $0.5M (opex)
3 Hire more crews	• Would allow us to hit project timelines	• Would exceed project capex budget by $1.6M

Depending on the level of detail your audience needs, you might want to create several slides to address each of these alternatives. In our case, we'll assume this level of detail is what's needed. Also, it's commonplace to put your recommended alternative last, since this supports a nice sequential flow for your material (in other words, your next few slides will be about the last thing covered on this slide).

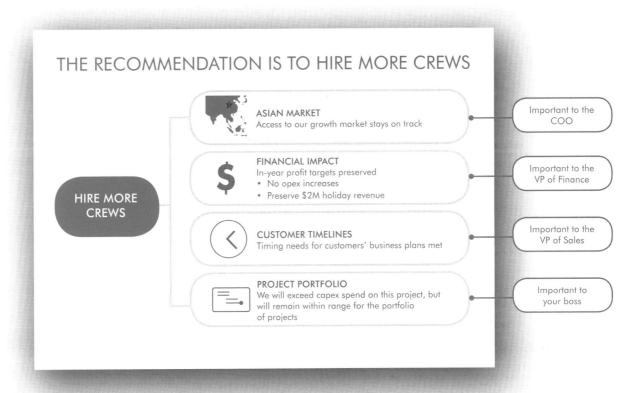

THE RECOMMENDATION IS TO HIRE MORE CREWS

HIRE MORE CREWS

ASIAN MARKET
Access to our growth market stays on track

Important to the COO

FINANCIAL IMPACT
In-year profit targets preserved
• No opex increases
• Preserve $2M holiday revenue

Important to the VP of Finance

CUSTOMER TIMELINES
Timing needs for customers' business plans met

Important to the VP of Sales

PROJECT PORTFOLIO
We will exceed capex spend on this project, but will remain within range for the portfolio of projects

Important to your boss

Let's pretend that, despite their pay grade, this group needs you to pick one of these alternatives and then explain why it's the best potential solution. This is a good time to link your recommendation back to those personal motivators each audience member has, in order to address each person's specific concerns. Above is an example of what this slide might look like.

IMPLEMENTATION PLAN

STREAM	PRIME	DETAILS	Q1	Q2	Q3	Q4
External crews	Jill	• Negotiate & sign contract • Train crews on safety and procedure	▬▬			
Purchase tools	Jan	• Determine what tools are needed vs. what are in place • Negotiate bulk purchase • Ship to site		▬		
Reassign internal workforce	Sarah	• Analyze where effectiveness of internal crews will be optimized • Review plans with labor relations • Reassign crews to new locations			▬▬	

KEY MILESTONES

April 1 – All necessary tools in place for external crews

May 1 – All four external crews begin work

Oct 20 – Construction completed

Now that you've wowed everyone with your ability to come up with a wonderful solution, let's show them how you plan to implement it. A great way to do this is with a simple Gantt chart, which we looked at in an earlier section. Here's an example of what this slide might look like.

And since you're not just a one-trick pony, let's provide a hint of what you're going to do as an encore by laying out the next few steps.

NEXT STEPS

- Follow up on feedback from this discussion
- Email weekly project status updates to this steering team
- Schedule monthly meetings to review project progress

MAKE-BELIEVE RAILWAY INC.

And there we have it. These are the detailed slides that are appropriate for emailing. If you end up presenting virtually and using a shared desktop, then you'll just set up your presentation so that the content on these slides builds one point at a time.

But what about the slides you're going to be using while you're presenting to the big kids? Since you're going to be in the room, let's just remove all of the detail that you're going to be speaking about. To help decide what to include, try just highlighting one or two key things, such as:

- The "so what" or key point you're trying to deliver.
- The big question you're asking for people's feedback on.
- A diagram that helps to explain a complex point.

Here's an example of what the slides you present in person might look like:

MAKE-BELIEVE RAILWAY INC.

STATUS REVIEW OF THE EXPANSION PROJECT

Your name
Date

WHY ARE WE HERE TODAY?

Decision on the expansion

WHAT THE LEADERS NEED TO KNOW ABOUT CURRENT STATUS

KEY DATA POINTS TO KNOW FOR THIS DECISION

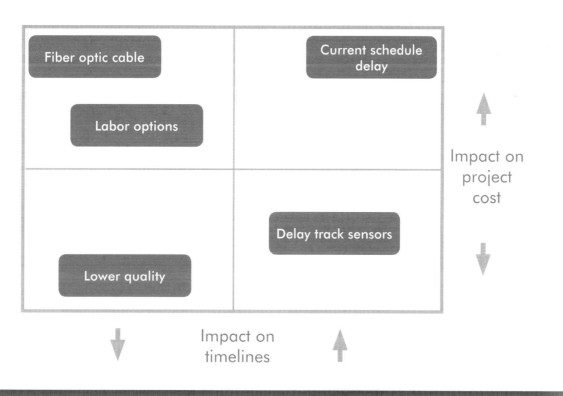

PROS & CONS OF THE 3 MAJOR ALTERNATIVES

1 Status Quo

2 Lower the rail quality

3 Hire more crews

THE RECOMMENDATION IS TO HIRE MORE CREWS

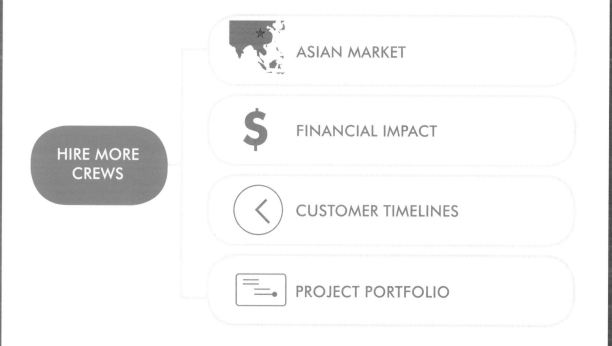

HIRE MORE CREWS

ASIAN MARKET

FINANCIAL IMPACT

CUSTOMER TIMELINES

PROJECT PORTFOLIO

IMPLEMENTATION PLAN

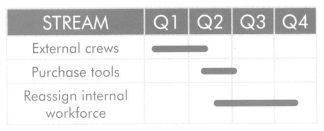

STREAM	Q1	Q2	Q3	Q4
External crews	▬▬			
Purchase tools		▬		
Reassign internal workforce		▬▬▬		

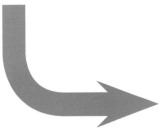

KEY MILESTONES

April 1 – Tools bought

May 1 – Crews start

Oct 20 – Construction done

NEXT STEPS

- Feedback
- Weekly update
- Monthly meeting

MAKE-BELIEVE RAILWAY INC.

So that's it.

If you're presenting in person, this would be a good time to take a bow, receive your ovation, and catch any roses being thrown in your direction.

We're all done! If you liked this book, then please tell all your friends. But as a gesture of respect for the presentation gods, please sacrifice this book by lighting it on fire and having your friends buy their own copies.

Hopefully you picked up a few tricks that will help you make slick slides. If you think you're pretty good now, prove it by uploading some of your best slides and making them available for sale at www.powerthroughpresentations.com. Who knows, you might even make a buck or two.

Further Reading

If you still want to dig deeper into different aspects of how to create great slides, you might want to check out a few of the titles referenced in this book.

slide:ology: The Art and Science of Creating Great Presentations, by Nancy Duarte. Published by O'Reilly Media, 2008.

Presentation Zen: Simple Ideas on Presentation Design and Delivery, by Garr Reynolds. 2nd edition. Published by New Riders, 2011.

Beyond Bullet Points: Using Microsoft PowerPoint to Create Presentations that Inform, Motivate, and Inspire, by Cliff Atkinson. 3rd edition. Published by Microsoft Press, 2011.

Acknowledgments

Once upon a time, Karen Radford put a young man on a plane and sent him to Asia to build some PowerPoint® slides. He was so afraid of soiling the bed on the assignment that he started reading a bunch of books on how to build great presentations, which was really the genesis of this book.

Over the years, the concepts were refined through the creation of thousands and thousands of slides. In 2011, some very smart people at TELUS were kind enough to share their PowerPoint® wisdom in a professional development series, which included Daryl Storey, Kristen Rasmussen, and Scott Perkins.

It was from their tips, tricks, and templates that the foundation of book was built.

Thank you all.

About the author

Andy received a Bachelor of Electrical Engineering degree but can't engineer his way out of a paper bag. He also has a business degree, with a double major in playing cards and shooting pool. So how was he to get ahead in this world with no discernible knowledge or skills?

Andy's answer was PowerPoint® presentations. Early on in his career he developed a reputation for being able to take complex topics and create simple, effective presentations. This ultimately evolved into his being a sought-after expert who develops material for large multinational organizations, which has taken him to the U.S., South Korea, the Philippines, and throughout Canada.

Andy currently works as a Director, Project Centre of Excellence with TELUS Communications in Vancouver, Canada.

At ECW Press, we want you to enjoy this book in whatever format you like, whenever you like. Leave your print book at home and take the eBook to go! Purchase the print edition and receive the eBook free. Just send an email to ebook@ecwpress.com and include:

Get the eBook free!

• the book title
• the name of the store where you purchased it
• your receipt number
• your preference of file type: PDF or ePub?

A real person will respond to your email with your eBook attached. Thank you for supporting an independently owned publisher with your purchase!